NO BAD DAYS

More Lives than a Cat

Jeff Covelle

Amazon

To my son Antony, who helped me through the days I would not have managed to get through by myself; and to Eileen, who restored the twinkle in my eye which I had lost, and rekindled the fire in my belly, when no other could.

CONTENTS

INTRODUCTION

Why have I written this book? I'm not a famous celebrity of cinema or television. I'm just an ordinary guy, but I've had quite an eventful life.

I've always thought that I would try my hand at writing a short story, one day, but never got around to it. I also thought my short story would be Science Fiction, as my two favourite authors are Isaac Asimov and Arthur C. Clarke. I never thought I would be writing an autobiography! It's my son I have to thank/blame for that. As he said, "What else do you have to do in Lockdown?".

It's currently February 2021 and the Covid19 virus is rampant in the United Kingdom, and the rest of Europe. I am confined to my home, except for food shopping and medical appointments, and I've finished building the LEGO Porsche car my son bought me for my last birthday!

My book is as true as I can possibly make it, but I am relying on my memory an awful lot! I can definitely say that everything in here is a truthful interpretation, and hopefully representation, of what happened. Events may have gotten a little out of order, but not enough to make any difference. I have also tried to add a little humour.

Some things may have been left out, but nothing has been added that didn't actually happen. Some of the left-out items are because I've forgotten about them, some because I feel they are too personal to publish, some because I find it too distressing to write about them, and others because they are too boring to record.

As I have no permissions from anyone mentioned in this book, I have not used any real surnames or specific addresses of people, other than my family. I've also forgotten some of the names of those mentioned, so I've just made them up, as I don't think names are really that important in the context of this book.

It is not my intention to upset or embarrass anyone.

So, enjoy the read!

Chapter One

Early Days

I arrived in this World at a pretty good time.

It was September 1945. The war in Europe had finished in May, and the war with Japan had ended just a month before. After six years of conflict, peace was finally here.

Definitely of a lower class family, I was the first child of the union between my parents. My father (Tony) was a French Canadian, who originated somewhere in the outback of Saskatchewan. English was not his first language, that being a weird version of the French language. He came from a large family, having six brothers. His education was none existent, and he left home when he was about sixteen or seventeen and joined the French Foreign Legion. It's not known how long he remained there, but he then went as a mercenary in the Spanish Civil War. (Don't know which side!). He never spoke of his brothers, other than to say they all died during World War II. He never even mentioned his parents to me, and the one time I raised the subject, he just told me they died when he was very young.

After the Spanish Civil War, he fought in the Second World War against the Japanese. He met my mother when he took leave in the UK in December 1944.

He was a tall man of about six feet one inch, quite slender, brushed back black hair (which in later years thinned considerably and turned white), a pencil thin moustache, piercing dark blue eyes and, many would say, quite handsome. He was very articulate and spoke with a slight accent, but miss-pronounced many words. He read poorly, and wrote even worse. I never saw him lose his temper.

My mother (Nancy) originated from somewhere in the Lake District, where she was "in service" in a large house there. Mother was about five feet seven inches tall, not thin, and definitely not fat, having quite a good figure. Her hair was dark brown, shoulder length, and had a natural curl. Her eyes were a deep dark brown. She was quite fiery, being very quick tempered by nature. Her parents died when she was a teenager, which is how she ended up "in service".

Mother lived in Sunderland, which is my home town, after meeting her first husband there sometime before the beginning of the Second World War. When I asked about her first husband, she told me he had perished in the War, going down with his ship in the Atlantic in the early years of the conflict. I learned more about this in my later life!

I inherited my mother's curly hair and my father's blue eyes and even temper.

Since both of my parents were not well educated, neither had good jobs!

My mother was a waitress in a café in the town centre, just outside the entrance to the railway station.

My father did almost anything to earn a living. My earliest recollection of his job was as an Ice Cream Man! He was also a painter and decorator, and latterly a used tyre dealer.

We lived in a rented half of a terraced house on the outskirts of town. We had the downstairs, which was a lounge, at the front of the house, a bedroom in the middle, and a kitchen to the rear. It had only the one front door from the main road which opened to a passageway, with our lounge to the right, and our bedroom door a little further along, about where the bottom of the stairs were. Further along the passageway, directly ahead, was our kitchen, and, just before it, a door to the right led into the back yard.

A young couple occupied the upper floor.

There was no bathroom, just an outside toilet at the bottom of the concrete backyard, next to the coal shed. The toilet was shared with upstairs: the coal shed was ours!

I shared the bedroom with my parents for all of the time we lived there.

As a very young child (before attending school) I remember very little. I recall it was always cold in the winter, food was very basic, but occasionally I had a treat of chocolate! Because the war had not long finished, many things were rationed, including chocolate. The quite small bar, I think it was four ounces, consisted of eight squares. My treat was one square which was cut into four pieces so I could savour it.

Probably the reason I love chocolate so much now, which is again rationed, but now because of health problems!

Sunday night was bath night. The bathtub hung on the wall in the yard when not in use. We all shared the water in the metal tub in front of the fire in the kitchen. Mother had the first bath, Dad followed, and I was last. By my turn the water was getting a little cool, so I had a top up with a kettle of hot water.

I do remember the trams going past our house, and my friend Chris and I making swords out of a six inch and a one-inch nail. The one-inch nail was laid across the six-inch nail, about one inch from the head of the large nail. Both nails were carefully placed on the tram track, and we just waited for the tram to come. If we were lucky the nails flattened and fused together, and we had a small steel sword we could have sword fights with, and hopefully draw blood. Good fun for young lads, but Mothers were not happy with blood stains on our clothes!

Since I was born in the second half of September, I was almost six when I started school. I was the oldest in my class.

My school was directly opposite our house. All I had to do was cross the road, and I was at the gate. As both my parents were at work before school started it was up to me to make sure I got there on time. I normally left home when I heard the whistle, and didn't quite make it on time if there was any traffic on the road. Consequently, I nearly always had additional homework as a punishment.

I attended school dinners as both of my parents were at work all day. The canteen was not on the school premises and it took about fifteen minutes for the convoy of children to walk there. After we had finished our lunch, we were left to our own devices to get back to school for the afternoon lessons. Lunch break was between noon and 1:30pm. A fifteen minute walk each way, and lunch took about half an hour to eat. Plenty of time you would think, but for a seven- or eight-year-old, it was not! I remember my friend George and I returning from lunch one day. As we walked past the brook,

"How about we look for newts?" George said.

"Sure thing." I said.

So, we did.

We arrived back at school just as it was finishing at 4pm. We did get into trouble!

One day, when I was about eight years old, there was a gale. I was at home with my mother, and it was quite cold so I was in the kitchen with my mother, who was cooking over the Victorian coal fired range we had. The wind was whistling through the badly fitting sash window, rattling the window pains to the point where I was sure they would fall out. Smoke was blowing back down the chimney depositing a fine layer of soot everywhere. Suddenly, there was a loud sound of creaking and the groaning of stressed timber.

"Run!" I heard my mother scream.

There was nowhere, and no time to run, so I dived under

the kitchen table.

The crashing sound was horrendous; the dust was choking; I was choking; I was petrified; I was sure I wet myself. Masonry was piling up around me and on the sturdy oak table above my head.

After what seemed like an eternity to me, the dust settled, and all I could hear was,

> "Jeffrey, Jeffrey, Jeffrey" being screamed by my mother.
>
> "Mam, I'm okay" I shouted, as she frantically started pulling the huge bricks and rubble away from the table, without much success.

Neighbours had seen and heard the commotion, had called the Fire Brigade, and were eagerly clawing at the rubble when I emerged some ten minutes later, unscathed and crying. The Fire Brigade arrived some ten minutes later, astounded that I had not been injured or killed.

The gale had blown over the chimney stack, which had crashed through the roof, then through the upstairs ceiling and floor, eventually ending up in our kitchen. It came through the middle of the ceiling, right above where I was. My Mother was at the side of the room putting something in the oven and managed to jamb herself into the corner of the room, only having enough time to shout to me to get out.

Luckily the people upstairs were not at home.

This was my first brush with death.

We were temporally rehoused for several months while the house was repaired, and in fact, we never actually returned to that house.

I've never been sure how it happened, or too sure how they could afford it, but the next house we lived in was bought by my parents! It was probably affordable because it was leasehold, and on a short lease as the area in which it stood was scheduled for redevelopment as part of the expansion of Sunderland College. The College eventually became a university.

Anyway, the house was huge and rambling. Quite a difference from our previous home. It was also very close to the town centre.

It was an end of terrace house, at the dead-end of a terrace of seven houses. It was three stories high, with a bathroom between the first and second stories. There were two large reception rooms, the kitchen and a small dining room annexed to the kitchen on the ground floor. Up a flight of about fifteen stairs, there was a small landing with a further two flights of about six stairs. One flight went to the bathroom (which had a radiator in it), the other flight went to the next floor, which had three bedrooms. From this floor there was another flight of about twenty stairs, which went up to two further rooms.

A massive house.

There was a large triangular shaped garden, the house being one side, a railway line on another side, and finally, the third side was a boundary wall for an abandoned and partially derelict Flour Mill.

A young boy's heaven!

Having a larger house, which I don't think my parents could really afford, meant we needed some more income, so my parents took in Lodgers.

The prestige room was the one at the front of the house with the bay window, below my bedroom, which was occupied by Cecil, a retired Merchant Seaman. He lived there for about eight years, and died there. Cecil was a huge man! Well over six feet tall and weighing about twenty-five stones, with a fat smiley face and bald head. He spent all day in his room watching cricket on his small black &

white television, only venturing out to visit the toilet or cook something in his large frying pan.

The two upstairs loft rooms were also rented out. One was occupied by Bill, a small, elderly looking wizened man with a sad face, who was a bus driver. He also lived there until he died, shortly after his retirement. The other loft room was occupied by Paddy, an Irish labourer, who was a typical stereotype. He looked like you would expect an Irish labourer to look. He was about 5'10", heavy set, only shaved about once a week, had black greasy hair, and came home drunk whenever he had enough money to do so, which was normally Friday, Saturday, and Sunday! He was still living there after I had left.

My father also reared chickens and turkeys. He had about twenty chickens, which provided us with ample eggs, and some to sell, and after their laying days were over, we would eat them for Sunday dinner.

There were about a dozen turkeys which were reared purely to be sold at Christmas, apart from the one we had for our Christmas Dinner.

Dad also became a dog breeder. Only Chow Chows. There were always Chow Chows running around the house, and a litter of pups about every six months.

Two things which really stick in my memory about my dad was the way he cut a loaf of bread, and rolling up his cigarettes.

Our bread came from the local baker, just up the road a little, and it was one of my tasks to go and get it. It was always a large square uncut crusty loaf, which I normally nibbled the corners off on my way back from the bakers. Dad always stood the bread end up and cut a slice off by cutting from right to left and not top to bottom, which I would consider to be the conventional way. Also, He buttered, or more often spread his dripping on the bread before he cut the slice off! I never saw anyone else ever do that.

He was also a heavy smoker, normally about sixty cigarettes a day, and he rolled his own. His tobacco was a mixture of Golden Virginia and a black twist tobacco, which is actually a chewing tobacco. He bought his tobacco for the week, roughly 75% Golden Virginia, 25% black twist, mixed it on a sheet of newspaper laid on the floor in front of the fire, and started hand rolling his cigarettes. He spent about two hours producing between 400 and 500 thin, spindly fags, which he kept in several dozen empty Golden Virginia tins. In the winter he sat with his back to the only fire we had, totally blocking the heat from reaching anyone else, until my mother screamed at him to move!

We hadn't lived there long when I suddenly, or it seemed to me, had a baby sister. This was Jacqueline, who, born in 1954, was nine years younger than I. I wasn't too happy about having a baby sister, but my father had always wanted a daughter, and absolutely doted over her. It never bothered me as I had made two new friends in the next street. John, who was a thin wiry lad, and Anthony, a chubby lad whose parents ran the local pub.

As most young lads, we had adventures with whatever was at hand. The railway line was one of our favourite play areas. It was quite a busy line, but mainly slow-moving freight trains. We used to run along behind and jump on, or in, the last truck. We would ride for about a mile and jump off on a slow bend, then do the same to get back home. Probably a little dangerous, but not when you are ten years old!

Our other favourite play area was the old Flour Mill. A huge four-story building with grain shoots littered around it, which made excellent slides. Our Favourite game was "Cops & Robbers". We played it American style, as we were armed with air pistols. We only used the plastic "slugs" as ammunition, but someone always went home with a big black bruise somewhere on their body. Anthony was the biggest, so was a better target, and consequently ended up with most bruises.

Our 'gang', Anthony, John and I, were always in conflict with another gang which lived in the street on the other side of the Flour Mill. This became more intense the nearer to Bonfire Night it got. My Dad allowed us to have a bonfire on the vegetable patch, and a lot of our gang's time during the school holidays was collecting fuel for this event.

The other gang used to mount raiding parties to steal our hard worked for bonfire fuel. There were rules regarding this! The other gang would only come into our garden if we were not around. If we were there, we had a stone fight, but our rivals never invaded or engaged in 'hand-to-hand' combat. The same happened when we raided their bonfire store, which was on an old bomb site in their street.

It always seemed to even out, and we both managed to have a decent size bonfire on November 5th.

I was still going to the same school as I was before we moved house, but it was now about a mile away. I went by bus, so was never late!

I managed to pass my 11+ examination and was transferred to Bede School, which was the local grammar school. This was even further away, being an even longer bus trip of almost two miles. The bus fare was one and a half pence each way, so I was given three pence a day by my parents. I normally spent the return fare on sweets at lunchtime and had to walk home! I made new friends at my new school, in particular Dick and Barry, who both became lifetime friends.

Barry, who lived about a half mile from me, was tall and thin and clever. He was the only one of the three of us who went to university.

Dick, who lived about two miles away, was short and mild mannered and eventually ended up as an engineer helping design the "Cornetto" production line for Unilever.

I seldom saw John and Anthony, who both moved out of the

area shortly after I started going to Bede school.

At my new (all boys) school, we did French language. I was very bad at it, and getting my dad to help made things even worse. His French was not school French! After taking French for four years, I was not even allowed to sit the mock O-Level exam, as I was told I would have embarrassed the school.

During our four days a week, 40-minute French lesson, I normally sat at the back of the class with two of my mates, Dick and Mickey. The teacher, "Pop" as we called him, was very short tempered, especially with me. I never did my French homework. He would go around the class asking questions relating to the previous day's homework.

"COVELLE", he shouted, glowering at me, "lamp post is..... ......?". I hadn't a clue! Time to improvise.

"La post de lamp", I responded.

His face went a very bright shade of purple as he screamed something incomprehensible, and threw the wooden blackboard rubber at me. I ducked and it hit the window behind me, breaking yet another of the small glass pains.

I concluded that this was not the correct translation!

I was responsible for the breakage of at least six panes of glass before I was forced to sit in the front row.

During one year, one of our French lessons was the last lesson on the Friday afternoon. The Jewish boys missed this lesson in the Winter as they had to leave school before it got dark. I tried to tell Pop I was Jewish, but he didn't believe me. I even asked if I could convert to Judaism, but was sent to the headmaster and caned, just for trying.

However, I was fairly good at most other subjects, and excelled at Mathematics, which I loved.

My maths teacher was "Boris". He looked like Albert Einstein, but with more hair, and just rattled through algebra, geometry, and trigonometry as if he was just chatting! Most of the class seemed at a loss, but it all seemed to make perfect sense to me.

I also enjoyed Engineering Drawing. I was slow but very methodical, and the teacher, "Dicky", always seemed impressed with my work.

Physics was another subject I quite enjoyed, but not the teacher, "Doc Jolly", who had quite a vicious streak in him. He liked to dig his knuckle into your upper arm if you got things wrong. He also took Biology, which I wasn't very good at, so I often got "knuckled".

I was sort of average in almost everything else, and was normally placed about 10th in our class of thirty pupils. Top in maths, bottom in French!

Each year had 120 pupils, split into four classes of 30 pupils, who were initially graded on entry based on each boy's 11+ exam result. I was in the third class, so actually my position was normally about 70th out of 120. Dick was in the same class as me, and normally about five places behind me. Barry was the clever one, being near the top of the second class, at about 35th.

My O'Level exam results were reasonable. I took seven, passing six, with a distinction in Maths, and a fail in Biology. As I mentioned earlier, I was not permitted to sit the French exam.

Dick passed five of his O-Levels; Barry, all eight.

I was not one of the best students, as I seemed to always be getting into trouble. The school owl was the subject of a high-spirited prank, in which I was involved, but never caught. Someone thought it would be fun if we painted the wise school owl pink, and put a school cap on him. The challenge being that the school owl was a stone sculpture about two feet tall, which was on the roof apex at the front of the school. It was four stories above the ground. The plotters formed a plan. It was late one summer's evening, and we had stayed late at school for one or other of the school clubs. We went up to the top floor of the school, armed with a tin of pink paint and a brush, and into the music room, which had a sloping ceiling. The ceiling had skylights. We opened one, climbed onto the roof, crawled up the tiles to the ridge of the roof, and scampered along to the owl at the end. Paint and brush were produced, the deed was done, and an old school cap was plonked on the owl's head!

Despite the in-depth enquiries carried out by the school staff over the following weeks, no one was ever caught for carrying out this disrespectful deed.

The last time I drove past the school, I could still see a hint of pink on the wise old owl.

A couple of years after starting Bede school, I was persuaded to join the scouts. As it happened the school had their own troupe, the Bedans, who met on Friday evenings. I enjoyed being a scout for about four years. The Bedans had a very old, dilapidated, wooden hut in an area at the boundary of the school and the local market garden.

Unfortunately, when unsupervised we used to have discus throwing contests, using dustbin lids as discuses. They did travel a lot further than we thought they would, and actually reached the greenhouses in the market garden! Six of the best from the head for us the following Monday!

The old scout hut was to be replaced with a new one, and the scoutmaster asked for volunteers to start dismantling the old one on Saturday. Four boys volunteered, of which I was one. Being the oldest (I was fifteen), I was put in charge.

We met in the scout hut the following morning, and started off kicking some of the side panels off. We were told to just pile up the old wood, and it would be removed the following week. After a couple of hours, we were getting a bit fed up with this, and did not seem to be making much progress, so I came up with what I thought was a brilliant idea. We could just burn it down, and there wouldn't even be much rubble to get rid of.

I managed to find a large old plastic bottle, and, just so I could make a good job of it, I walked ten minutes down the road to a petrol station and bought a half gallon of petrol. I duly arrived back at the scout hut, sprinkled the petrol as liberally as a half-gallon could be sprinkled, borrowed a match from one of the boys who was a smoker, and threw a piece of lighted paper into the scout hut.

There was a huge bang and flames leapt out of the doorway and windows. The old dry wooden hut burst into flames. It was a magnificent sight, and was still burning when the Fire Brigade arrived twenty minutes later! To my disappointment, they put the fire out, rather than letting it do its job.

At school next Monday morning I was threatened with expulsion, but got away with six of the best from the headmaster. The scoutmaster told me not to return to the troupe. I never even got the one shilling and sixpence back, which I paid for the petrol.

It was about this time I got my first bicycle. Barry and Dick both had bicycles, and I had never even ridden one at the age of fifteen. One of Barry's friends had a one for sale. Unfortunately, it was £2 and I only had £1. My Dad came to the rescue and "loaned" me the £1, which I never repaid.

It was Friday after school when I got the bike, and Barry showed me how to ride. We decided that the three of us, and another friend, Mickey, would cycle to Durham the next day and go on the boats.

We set off early on Saturday morning, and I hadn't got the hang of balance and gear changes, but eventually we got to the riverside in Durham. I was knackered. It was thirteen miles! We went to the boat hire man and hired two small rowing boats for an hour. It was two shillings (10 pence), plus a five shillings (25 pence) deposit. It wasn't very exciting rowing around, so we decided to have a game of "boat jousting".

We rowed as fast as we could towards each other, then as we passed each other we raised our oars and used them as lances. It was a great game until we got it a little wrong. Dick and I managed to hit Barry and Mickeys boat broadside. They were caught unprepared, stumbled about the boat, and fell in the water as the boat overturned and was floating with just the keel protruding from the river. They both swam to the bank, but the boat drifted to the middle of the river and was slowly swept downstream. Dick and I rowed to the river bank near Barry and Mickey who were taking their clothes off and wringing them out. We didn't know what to do, feeling sure the boatman would call the police when we told him about the accident.

We decided to just sit on the banks of the river in the sun for a couple of hours to let the clothes dry out a little bit, before abandoning the remaining boat which we tied to a tree. We then went back to the boathouse by a circuitous route to bring us back to the back of the boat yard, where we picked up our bikes and quickly hurried off. we logically assumed that our lost deposits would cover any damage or inconvenience, after all, that's what the deposit was for.

It was a tiring thirteen-mile cycle home, especially for me, as a novice cyclist. We often went out to a Youth Club on a Saturday night, but it was an early night that Saturday!

During the school summer holiday, just before my sixteenth birthday, Dick and I decided to hitchhike to London, camping on the way and staying at whatever overnight stops we could find. We planned on taking a week to do this. After all, it was only 280 miles, so two good hitches would get us there in two days, and the same would get us back.

We started off late on a Monday morning. We had a small two-man ridge tent, a couple of ground sheets, a sleeping bag each, and a few utensils.

"Are we ready to go?", I said to Dick.

"Sure we are." he said, "Let's get to our first hitch!".

We had decided the way to go. Straight down the A690 to the A1, then A1 all the way to London.

From Dicks house it was about half a mile to the A690, and after walking for about two hours we got a lift from a lorry driver. Not quite as far as we would have liked, as he was only going to Darlington. This was less than 30 miles, but was on the A1. It was now around 3pm. The next lift should get us almost to London, if we were lucky.

We didn't get another lift that day, and after walking another twelve miles or so, to Scotch Corner, we decided to call it a day, as it was about 7pm. We thought we would have something to eat and find somewhere to put the tent up. There was, and probably still is, a pub at Scotch Corner.

I said to Dick,

"I can't be bothered to find a shop, buy some food, then cook it. How about we just pop in this pub for something to eat, as we haven't even found a camp site yet?"

"Fine by me," Dick said, "and maybe have a pint of beer."

I could pass for eighteen, as I was already shaving, and had a weeks' worth of bum fluff on my chin.

"Okay" I responded, "but just a quick one, as we've got to find somewhere to pitch the tent."

We had some food in the pub, and too much beer for a couple of young lads. We don't know what time it was when we left the pub, but it was dark.

We weren't sure of our bearings when we left the pub. We walked a little way with the road on our right. It seemed to be a bit of a built-up area on our left, but was quite dark on the other side of the road. We were a little unsteady on our feet, but walked across the tarmac road and came to a grassed area.

"This looks fine to me", Dick said.

"It will do", I replied, "but it's too dark to see to put the tent up. I can only see some light shining in the distance."

We just got the ground sheets and sleeping bags out, snuggled in, and using the rolled up tent as a pillow, promptly went to sleep.

Dick woke up first.

"Yuk." he said, "What's that on your face?"

I stirred. Brushed my hand across my brow, just to discover a large snail was crawling across it.

"Bugger!", was my reply, followed by. "I need a pee!"

There must be a hedge or something further down the field. I stood up. I looked around me in amazement.

"Dick, stand up!"

He did. We both stood there looking about. We were in the middle of a large roundabout, which was on the A1! It had a dip in the middle, so we couldn't see the traffic until we stood up.

We rapidly packed our gear and got on the road. After walking for another four hours towards London (only about another 220 miles to go) without anybody stopping for us, we crossed to the other side of the road and caught the next bus home.

As with most children of my day, it was customary to do chores for your parents to earn your pocket money. One of my biggest chores, at the age of fifteen, was to clean the windows in our house. There was a lot! Three stories high, and end of terrace. I was expected to clean all the windows, inside and out. It normally took me about four hours.

Most of the windows were the sash type, where the top half could be slid down, and the bottom half slid up so that the outside glass could be reached from inside of the house. I had been doing this for about a year, and was getting quite quick and competent at it. One day, cleaning my bedroom window, I got it wrong! I used to sit on the window ledge, facing in, with my legs in the house and my body outside of the house. Just this once, I overstretched, and fell from the second floor onto the rock garden below. I was rushed to hospital, which was only a mile away, by ambulance.

I had done some damage to my back and bashed my head on the rocks. I was told I was lucky to be alive, and even more lucky to not be crippled. A week in the hospital, followed by a month wearing some sort of harness, and I was fine, although I still have a couple of damaged discs and vertebrae.

My second close call with death!

Although my O-Level results were not great, they were good enough for me to go on to my A-Levels.

I had decided on the three subjects I was going to take, Applied Mathematics, Pure Mathematics, and Physics. I had aspirations of being an Architect, if I got good A-Level results, and gained a university place. Unfortunately, this was not to be.

My Father, at this time, had a tyre repair business. One day he was replacing the exhaust on his van when the jack collapsed, trapping him underneath, and causing serious injury to his back and right shoulder. This meant he was unable to work for about six months. There was no way we could manage on my mother's wage as a waitress, and my father received no sickness or injury payments, so I had to go to work. This was on the understanding that I could do my A-Levels a year later, which never happened.

This is when I learned that my dad was actually not a legal resident of the UK. After the end of the War, he just decided to stay. He had no National Insurance, nor was he known to the National Health or the Taxation Authorities. I guess he was an Illegal alien!

He had always said,

> "I'm looking after us. I'll take nothing that I haven't earned.", and he was true to his word.

He gave nothing to the State, nor did he take anything from it.

Barry stayed on to do his A-Levels. Dick left school and took a job with British Rail in the ticket office in the Sunderland Central station.

And so, I entered the World of work.

Chapter Two

And so to Work

It was only a few weeks after I had taken my school exams that I was in the job market. It was August 1962, a month before my seventeenth birthday. I had resigned myself to the fact that I would not be going back to school, and being an Architect was now just a past dream. Perhaps I could be a Technical Draftsman? I knew that shipyards had draftsmen, and qualifications were earned by doing an apprenticeship. I checked with the biggest shipyard in Sunderland, just to be told that vacancies were limited, and anyway, I was too old!

Apprenticeships were only given up to the age of sixteen and a half.

In 1962 about 90% of work in the Sunderland area was either in the shipyards, or the coal mines. I was determined I would work in neither. Within a week I managed to get a job with Jobling, (the UK maker of 'Pyrex' glassware, under licence from Corning in the USA). I was a Junior Statistical Clerk, otherwise known as a tea boy. I was paid the princely sum of £4.62p a week. I gave my mother £4.12p, and was able to squander the remaining 50p however I wanted to.

The work was boring and repetitive, and consisted mainly of copying sales figures from a monthly sales sheet into a loose-leaf folder which was a detailed list of each piece of glass sold, and which company bought it. This was used to forecast sales and inform the factory as to which product line to make for the coming three months.

If there was a demand in Boots the Chemist for Harvest design 2-pint casserole dishes, I knew about it!

Also, one of the old (she was 23) typists in the typing pool fancied me, and I was shy and petrified of her.

I lasted eight months before quitting.

By this time my father had recovered enough to start work again.

I looked about to see if I could find something which was a bit more interesting, and paid a bit more money. I started my next job on Monday after leaving my old one on Friday!

My new job was as a Quality Control Paper Tester at Hylton Paper Mill, which was about five miles from my home. That was two bus rides and a ten-minute walk from home. About 40 minutes. Not too bad, you would think, but it was shift work, and the timings were not good. For night shift I was at work an hour early, and had to wait an hour in the morning for the first bus, or it was a 90-minute walk home.

However, the pay was good. Including my shift allowance, I was earning over £7 a week. I overcame the travel problem by buying an old Lambretta motor scooter, my dad lent me the £15, and I paid him back at £1 a week. I now had £1.50p a week for myself, plus a little more when I worked overtime at the weekends.

A Paper Mill is, or was for me in 1963, a strange and dangerous place to work. I worked in the laboratory (even wore a white coat), and my job, after one week's on-the-job training, was to test the quality of the paper after manufacture. Each type of paper had a specification sheet with tests designed to ensure the paper met that specification as each roll was made.

I would go into the machine house as each roll came off the machine (there were three machines) and take a sample. Unfortunately for me, the workers were on bonus, which they didn't get if a roll of paper was not up to specification. During night shift I was the only person in the laboratory, and felt vulnerable at times. The fact that about half of them had at least one finger missing didn't seem to help.

"How's the last test?", asked Doug.

"It's a bit rough on the left side", I replied.

"How's the last test?", repeated Doug, as he snipped off two of my shirt buttons with his knife.

"I'll let it go this time Doug, just make sure it's okay for the next roll", I countered.

Quality Control at its sharpest!

The guy who followed me on shift was almost always late, and I could not leave until he arrived. He was called Ray, but the workers called him 'one-blank' because he only had one eye. When he did arrive, the first thing he did was take his false eye out, then sit down and have a cup of tea. When it was busy, I had to continue working well past the end of my shift, until he came out of the Testers Room.

I recall that one day I got quite annoyed with him, so I hid his glass eye before I left. It took him an hour to find it, as I'd hidden it in a jar of pickled onions. The frequency of his lateness reduced after that.

Winter in the North-East of England on a motor scooter was not good. I had only owned my scooter for about six months, and it was an icy winters night as I set out for work at 10:30pm for my 11:00pm start.

Once off the main road, there was a minor road which ran for the last half mile along the edge of the River Wear before the Paper Mill. There was a narrow footpath along the side of the road, and a short wall about three feet high alongside the path. The other side of the wall was a six-foot drop into the River Wear.

I didn't even notice the icy patch on the road until I hit it. The wheels of my scooter spun momentarily before my Lambretta fell on its side. I was thrown off as the scooter continued to travel towards the kerbside. It mounted the path and did a dainty pirouette, before committing suicide by throwing itself over the wall into the river. I continued the next few hundred yards to work on foot.

I never saw my Lambretta again!

As my insurance was only third-party fire and theft, I reported it as stolen the next day, and in due course, I was paid £9.50p by the insurance company.

It was about this time that 'one-blank' left the paper mill, and a replacement was being sought. My friend Dick was getting a bit fed up with his job at this time. He was now the (only) ticket clerk at a small station at Seaburn, which is several miles from Sunderland Central. Dick lived on one of the outlying estates of Sunderland. To get to work at Seaburn in time for the first passenger train at 6am, he had to get up at 4am, get one of the few night buses to Sunderland Central, then get a freight train which dropped him off at Seaburn. He only worked until 1:30pm, but it was six days a week. He was paid £4.50p a week.

I suggested Dick to my boss as a replacement. Charlie didn't want to spend money on advertising the job, so he agreed to interview Dick. At this point I thought I had better mention it to Dick!

Dick was a bit hesitant when I mentioned it. He was never much of a daredevil, however the lure of £7 a week was too much to pass up. And, he'd practically got the job after the build up I had given him!

He did get the job, and joined me as a Paper Tester, although we never actually worked together.

With the regular weekend working overtime I was doing, I could afford a girlfriend, and a replacement motorcycle.

My first girlfriend was Brenda. She was slightly taller than I, skinny, with sharp features, and long hair. Our 'relationship' lasted about a month. She wanted to go out with her girlfriends on a Saturday night, and didn't like motorcycles!

My second, after a respectable break of four weeks, was Lynda. Lynda was short with a bit more meat on her. Something to cuddle! She had short hair and deep blue eyes and .... she liked motorcycles, and loved being my pillion at the weekend. I had now bought a 'proper' motorcycle, it was a BSA 250cc C15, on which I passed my driving test. I had the BSA for about six months, Lynda for about half that time.

It was at the Paper Mill where I first met Judi, my wife to be. I came in to work one Monday afternoon for my evening shift, and the regular office girl wasn't there. Judi was.

The laboratory where I worked had an office, where the boss, Charlie, sat. Next to his office, separated by a clear glass window, was the office where his secretary sat, and where all the paper manufacturing specification documentation was kept. Both offices had clear glass windows, with wooden doors, overlooking the laboratory. I couldn't miss her, as I could see her from my workstation.

Judi was very well proportioned, to my eye, about 5'7", long dark brown hair, brown eyes, and a beautiful smile. This was her first job, having left school at fifteen, and spending two years at secretarial college.

I was immediately drawn to her, but too shy to actually approach her, other than a casual greeting.

Dick knew of my interest in Judi. He would say,

> "Ask her out, you big jessie". (A Northern term for a wimp.)
>
> "I'm not really sure", I'd respond.
>
> "Go on", he'd continue, "You're like a big girl's blouse." (Means the same as jessie.)

I 'ummed' and 'ahed', and did nothing.

Dick, for probably the first time in his life, took control. He had asked Judi out for me! He arranged for us to go to the cinema on Saturday evening, and we would meet outside the cinema at 7pm. To my astonishment, she accepted the invitation given by proxy.

I wasn't going to see Judi before Saturday, as I was on night shift. It was a cold winter's evening in late 1963 and on my way to the cinema I had never been so nervous as I had been before. I was certain Judi wouldn't turn up, but I had to go to check. I even put my (only) suit on! She turned up. I was over the moon. She felt the same way about me as I did about her. We sat in the back row, and I've no idea what the film was. I took her home on the bus afterwards, and we kissed goodnight, before I skipped the whole two miles back to my home.

Judi's father had died of lung cancer at the age of 37 when Judi was only five years old. She lived with her mother, who was in her early fifties, and bedridden with arthritis and some other underlying health problems which I never heard about. Judi's great aunt Lottie, who was in her seventies, also lived with them to help Judi look after her mother. Apart from the small widow's pension her mother received, and her great aunt's old age pension, Judi was the sole breadwinner. She earned £4 a week.

I started dating Judi on a regular basis, and after about three months we became intimate. I was eighteen and half, a virgin, and Judi was seventeen.

I also upgraded my motorbike, selling my BSA 250cc to Dick, and buying a BSA 650cc Super Rocket. I loved both Judi and my BSA! Judi also loved being my pillion passenger, screaming in my ear as we hit the "ton" tearing down the A19 to visit Judi's aunt and uncle in Peterlee.

Judi had made a new friend at the Mill. She was called Valerie, and was an office worker in another department. Val was very attractive! She was about 5'3", slender, with shoulder length dark brown hair, and a very pleasant smile. She also had a boyfriend, Norman! Norman was a pleasant unassuming guy, slightly built, and a few inches taller than Val. We ended up as good friends, and often went out together. The wrestling in Newcastle on a Saturday night was one of our favourites, until someone told Val that it may not be as genuine as she thought it was! Norman also had a car, an Austin A40, which was also a bonus. Val and Judi both got quite excited at the wrestling, with favourite phrases, such as,

"Tear his arm off and hit him with the soggy end!"

"Rip his head off!"

"Jump on his face!"

"Break his back!"

And other ladylike expressions of support.

At work I was asked if I would like to move on from being a Paper Tester, as there was a vacancy for a Trainee Instrument Technician. They said I could have 'day release' from work for one day a week, to go to college to get qualified, if I wanted. I jumped at the chance. It was day work so I lost my shift allowance, but a small salary increase helped to offset most of that, and I was now being paid £8 a week. There was also some overtime, if there was weekend testing of any new installations taking place.

I was able to spend a lot more time with Judi now.

I recall one of my very first tasks was making perspex instrument covers out of sheet perspex. The drill slipped and I ended up drilling a hole in my thigh. It hurt, and bled a lot, and hurt even more at the hospital where the nurse picked out pieces of denim with her tweezers before stitching it up.

I did learn a lot from my on-the-job training and my college day release. Most of the work I did was electro-mechanical, which was calibration, set up, routine maintenance, and servicing of monitoring and control equipment. With the coming of the 'transistor', things got more interesting and a lot more technical. The guy in charge of the Technical Department had a university degree and enjoyed this 'leading edge' technology, so no one else got to do much, other than what they were told. I found the work I did interesting, but not challenging.

At school, I wasn't really into sports. I disliked football, cricket, and any athletics which involved running. I quite liked rugby, shot put, high jump, and pole vault. However, the thing I was really good at was gymnastics, and was even a respected member of the Gym Club at school.

I took a liking to Wrestling about this time, starting off doing a bit of Cumberland wrestling, then onto Greco-Roman. My Dad knew a guy (he seemed to know a guy for everything) who was a wrestling coach, and said it would be good to be trained by him. Seemed like a good idea, so I went along to see Digger (he was Australian) at his gym, which was a room in a recently closed railway station, only about a mile from our house.

Digger took me in the ring and put me through my paces. There wasn't much I could show him, but he showed me a few moves I hadn't come across before, which I quite quickly mastered.

I was getting a bit concerned that I could not afford to join his classes, and said,

> "Before we go any further, Digger, what do you charge for tuition?"
>
> "No charge", was the answer.
>
> "No charge!", I responded in disbelief.
>
> "Why would I charge you?" Digger said.
>
> "How do you keep in business, then?", said I.
>
> "Hasn't your dad explained?", was Digger's response.
>
> "Explained what?", I said with a bewildered look.

Digger went on to explain that he was training people like me to join his Professional Wrestling enterprise.

Dad had neglected to mention this!

All I had to do was buy a pair of wrestling boots and he would train me, with several others, to learn Professional Wrestling. And .... I didn't pay him, he paid me, when I was sufficiently trained to wrestle publicly.

I said I'd think about it, and let him know in a couple of days. I was really quite keen to have a go, but as I was paying monthly for my motorbike, I didn't have £10 spare to have my wrestling boots made!

Dad came to the rescue, lending me the money for the boots, which I could pay back when I started wrestling for money.

It took two weeks to have my boots made after my fitting. That week I started my training. Two evenings and a Sunday morning.

After six weeks we were told we were proficient enough to wrestle publicly.

Publicly, we discovered, was anywhere someone was willing enough to pay for us. Digger had purchased a wrestling ring which came apart and would fit into the back of Diggers van. Mostly, it was Working Men's Clubs for the Sunday lunchtime session.

I really enjoyed it, and I was paid £4 a session, which was about half my day job weekly earnings.

Contrary to popular belief, the bouts were not rehearsed. We were told who would win, and how. For example, a submission for Jeff in the third round. There were normally eight of us, so there were normally four bouts, and maybe a 'tag' match, which was two on each side.

Wrestling does consist of sequences of well-rehearsed moves, so it is advisable to 'go with the flow'. One of the guys I was matched with decided to break the sequence at the wrong time, which resulted in me dislocating his shoulder. It was also very important to learn how to fall without hurting yourself, but making it look spectacular.

I was normally a good guy. Mainly because I was very athletic, having a gymnastics background, and I was quick and able to showboat a lot.

Occasionally, I was cast as a bad guy. I was 'The Hood', and wore a hood throughout the match. As a bad guy you are expected to do a bit of cheating, and blind side the referee (who was Digger) with a bit of gouging and the odd punch, rather than the forearm smash.

I only wrestled for about a year, as I was thrown out of the ring and landed badly, breaking a bone in my heel. I was never able to wrestle again after that.

Much to my mother's disapproval, once Judi and I had become intimate, I spent a lot of time at her house. Her mother was bedridden, and elderly aunt Lottie went to bed before 9pm. Judi normally went to bed at about 10:30pm, and I often joined her.

My mother did not allow me a front door key, she left the door unlocked if I was at work, but I had to be in by 11pm if I was not at work. Initially, this proved to be a problem, but I overcame it. I started coming in just before locking up time, and going upstairs to bed. My mother would shout up the stairs if she heard me, but I didn't reply. The next thing I heard from her was at 7:30am, if I was not downstairs to go to work.

I had a cunning plan!

I used to stay with Judi until about 6am, leave quietly, (which meant pushing my motorbike down the street before starting it) and going home.

When I got to the end of the street where I lived, I switched off my bike and pushed it down the street into the small shed where I kept it. I then climbed the drainpipe to the flat top of the downstairs bay window, which was the sash window to my bedroom. I always left the window unlocked, so I just had to raise the window, and get into bed! I almost got back too late of several occasions, opening the window as my mother was calling up the stairs. I must have done this for about six months and my mother never knew. I think maybe my father suspected, but he never said anything.

Judi's mother was in her mid-50's when she died in 1965. I wanted to move in with Judi, but there was disapproval from her aunt and uncle, her great aunt Lottie, and a lot more than disapproval from my mother! Even so, I did spend most evenings and nights with her, and I did contribute towards the £1.25p a week rent on her house.

I had been an Instrument Technician for about eighteen months in late 1965, and had completed the first year of my two-year training as an "Industrial Measurement & Control Technician" at the college in Middlesbrough, and had started the second year. I was still being paid £8 a week, and was told that I might get a rise after I had completed the course in Middlesbrough in the following August. I wasn't too happy about that, so I looked around for another job. I got one as a Science Laboratory Technician in a Secondary school.

It was a salaried position, and I started on a middle grade, which commanded a salary of £550 per annum, (about 40% more than I was paid at the Mill), and three weeks holiday instead of the two weeks I was getting at the Paper Mill. A great move for me.

The only drawback was that I could only have my day at college if I made up the time at work. I did this by working late the day before college to ensure everything was set up for the day I was not around, and working a Saturday morning.

Judi and I decided we should think about getting married, but were told we were too young. We were "unofficially" engaged. This was because we didn't want all the hassle we would get if we let people know, and I couldn't afford an engagement ring anyhow!

I enjoyed my new job, which mainly consisted of setting up scientific experiments in the chemistry and physics labs, and looking after the small animals in the biology laboratory. These were mice, rats, frogs, and locusts! I also looked after the school projector, and was the projectionist for the whole school, showing such show stopping films as; The Life-cycle of the Frog, The Amoeba and other Single Cell Animals, The Nitrogen Cycle, The Story of Bread, and, Safety in a Chemistry Laboratory. Gripping stuff!

I was the only lab technician in the school, and I did have my own room. This was quite good, as I could catch up with my college work during the quiet spells. I also quite liked still life drawing.

In May 1966, Judi and I decided to get married in the late July. My mother went through the roof! Basically, she was jealous of Judi and didn't want me to leave home.

"She (Judi) has trapped you into this, hasn't she?", my mother shouted at me when I told her.

"No, I want to get married", I retorted.

"You've got her pregnant, haven't you?", was her next accusation.

"No, not yet", was my rebuttal.

"She's only after you to look after her because her mother died", mother spat out at me.

"We love each other, and that's a good reason to want to live together", I responded.

I walked out of the room, very annoyed and disappointed at my mother's attitude. I never forgave her for that. However, she was probably right about Judi being pregnant. Although neither of us knew, Judi was probably one or two weeks pregnant at this time! We definitely knew she was when we got married in Late July of that year.

I told my father who thought it was great.

"I'll have two daughters now!", he said gleefully.

Our marriage was not a lavish affair on that Friday 22nd July. Judi did not have a bridal gown, just a very smart white suit. I bought a very cheap new suit and black shoes for the occasion. We were married in the local Methodist Church, which Judi's aunt Lottie attended, and the reception was held in the church hall. Sandwiches and cakes, and a small Wedding Cake. No alcohol, of course!

Barry, who was now a student of Liverpool University, was my Best Man. My sister, Jacqueline, and her cousin Joyce, were Judi's bridesmaids, and Judi's uncle Stan gave the bride away. Stan's Jaguar car was used as the wedding car. There were about ten guests, all from Judi's side of the family, except Dick.

My Dad paid for the wedding, and Judi's Uncle Stan paid for the weeks Bed & Breakfast we stayed in for our Honeymoon in Wales.

We had planned on leaving for our Honeymoon the following morning, but my motorbike had broken down, or that's what I'd told everyone! My Dad managed to scrape together enough money for the train fare, so we went the day after.

It was the first time either of us had been to Wales. We got on the train in Sunderland in the early hours of Sunday. It took about eight hours to reach our destination. We eventually found our B&B accommodation, said hello to the Owners, and went to our room to unpack. We then thought we would go to the local pub for a meal and a couple of drinks. We definitely needed both. It was a long boring train journey, and we had only a few sandwiches and a few cups of coffee all day.

The local pub was only a hundred yards down the road, and we were both ready for a pint and a steak pie! Opening time was six o'clock, which was exactly the time we left our room. By five past six we were at the pub.

"It's a bit dark in there", I said to Judi, as I peered through the window.

"It's early. There's nobody in yet.", Judi replied, "After all, it's quite rural here."

"We'll give them five minutes." I responded.

We gave them five minutes, then ten minutes, then after fifteen minutes I started banging on the door. No reply. I banged again, only louder and harder this time.

"Yes, what do you want?", a figure leaning out of an upstairs window snapped at us.

"Some food and beer", I responded. "What time do you open?"

"Monday.", was the response, as he slammed the window closed!

We had just learned that pubs didn't open on Sundays in Wales!

As we were on Honeymoon, there was quite a lot of "in bed" activity! It was a rather old metal framed bed which had casters on each leg. It used to jump about the floor, and squeak like Hell.

The waitress seemed to give us some odd looks when we went down for breakfast. We hadn't realised that our room was directly above the dining room. This rather embarrassing situation was cured by placing one of Judi's slippers under each of the front legs of the bed, and my slippers under each of the rear legs. A very efficient silencing system. It was just as well really, as it rained almost every day, so we were always last in for breakfast, just before they stopped serving.

Honeymoon over, and back home for us.

I officially moved in with Judi, and was now the man of the house. Aunt Lottie decided to move out and went to live with one of her friends nearby. I did ask her to stay, but she said,

> "What reason is there for me to stay any longer?"
>
> "You are always welcome to visit any time", I responded, thinking, quite wrongly as it turned out, that I would probably not see her again!

My first task when we returned from Wales, was to repair my motorbike, which took a bit of doing.

My motorbike hadn't actually broken down. I had been involved in an accident, but not told anyone.

It had been a couple of days before I got married when the accident happened.

For relaxation I occasionally liked to go for a bit of a 'burn up' on my bike with a couple of friends who had big bikes. We were riding down the main A19, at about 90mph, enjoying the exhilaration of the wind blowing in our faces. We were overtaking a coach. I was just about level with the front of the coach; there was a loud bang, and I lost control of my bike, totally! My front tyre had just exploded. The only thing I recall clearly was my bike and I being hit by the front of the coach. I went down. My bike shot off to the side, and the coach went over me. I could hear his brakes squealing as I looked above me at the underside of the coach. He had gone completely over me before he stopped. The differential in the rear axle had just missed me as the coach passed over me. I was left lying in the middle of the road.

I had only a few scratches and bruises, but my crash helmet was cracked all down one side. I was a little shocked and dazed. The police and ambulance were called, I was checked over in the ambulance, and allowed to go home. One of my friends took me home, and they both arranged to collect my bike and get it repaired while I was away on Honeymoon.

I never told Judi about my third brush with death.

We did, of course, know by this time that Judi was pregnant. We chose not to tell anyone just yet.

Judi had a lot of problems with her pregnancy. She had very high blood pressure for most of the time, and was admitted to hospital twice.

My parents were obviously aware of the upcoming birth or our child, but my mother was still very cold towards Judi; my father was over the moon!

About three weeks before Judi was due to give birth, we were having a Saturday night at home. Dick had come round to visit, as he often did, and we were having an Indian take-away curry. Right in the middle of watching 'Perry Mason' on TV, Judi shouted out,

"I'm having my baby!".

"You can't be", I exclaimed, "It's not due for another three weeks yet!".

"I've got the pains, now!", screamed Judi.

Dick went white and sat there quiet as a mouse, saying nothing.

"I've got to get to the hospital, now!", Judi blurted out.

"Okay", said I, "We will go now."

Turning to Dick I said,

"We'll go in your car. It will be quicker than an ambulance".

I didn't have a car, and the nearest phone box was ten minutes away.

Dick and I bundled Judi into the front seat of his Hillman Imp, and I got in the back seat. The hospital was about ten minutes' drive away, and Dick panicked all the way. When we arrived, Judi was put on a trolley and wheeled in. I was not allowed in. Dick and I waited for about two hours before a nurse appeared to tell us Judi was not giving birth yet and was not in labour, but was being kept in for observation.

We were told to go home and call back the following morning.

It was about midnight, so Dick and I went back to my house, warmed up the curry we had just started three hours before, and had a couple of beers! Dick went home at about 2am, and I went to bed.

The next day I went to the hospital (on my motorbike) to see what was happening with Judi. I was allowed to visit her, but I was told she would be remaining in hospital for the next three weeks until the baby was born.

Antony was born two days later, in late January 1967, two days after his mother's twentieth birthday!

I was not allowed to attend the birth, as was the custom at that time. There were many complications, which I, as the father, was never told about! Judi was in hospital a further week. While Judi was in hospital, I had to get things ready for the baby. As Antony was early, we had nothing! Not even any nappies. I was given a huge list of things to get, including a cot, a pram and a carry cot. My Dad bought the cot, and I managed to get a cheap second-hand pram and carrycot.

I also needed some family transport. Although I had passed my car driving test a year earlier, I could not afford a car. So, I traded in my 1959 650cc BSA Super Rocket motorcycle for a 1956 600cc BSA B21, with a sidecar. I checked first that the carry cot would fit in the sidecar!

On her discharge, we were told that Judi should not risk having any more children, as they would certainly die, and she probably would also.

Judi was on "The Pill" for the next two years, but she reacted badly to it, so I took the only other option there was available, which was a vasectomy! Quite a big decision for a guy who was only twenty-two years old, especially as I was told the operation was irreversible. Unfortunately, as I had discovered three years earlier, I was allergic to gossamer!

The operation was not a major thing in itself, and I actually went to the local hospital during my lunch hour to have it done. I was more embarrassed than anything else, especially when the nurse just taped my willy up out of the way so the surgeon could get to work. Operation took less than five minutes, and I was told to take it easy for the rest of the day. It did ache in the afternoon though!

At this time our family transport was my motorbike with its sidecar. I never liked it, neither did Judi. Definitely not like riding a motorbike without a sidecar. I decided that a three-wheeler car might be a good idea. I looked at an Isetta bubble car, but it was far too small. I had a friend who had a Reliant Robin, but they kept turning over, so I didn't think that would be good with a baby on board. I decided on a Bond. Probably the worst car I have ever had. It had a 125cc Villiers 2-stroke engine, and absolutely no power at all with two adults, a baby, and lots of baby accessories. The worst thing was if it stalled at the traffic lights. It had a kick starter which was under the bonnet, so if it was raining you got soaked, as everyone behind tooted their horns and shouted abuse at you!

Judi wasn't too bothered about family transport until I passed my driving test and we could afford a four wheeled car. I bought another motorbike, as transport to work. It was a Triumph T120 650cc Bonneville, which I did like a lot.

Another mouth to feed, and Judi wasn't working now. I needed to earn more money. My job as a lab technician was with the local Education Authority, and salary increases were annual and small, and because I worked in a school, I could not progress to the next grade. I was almost at the top of the grade, which was about £650 per annum. Time to look around again. I saw a similar type of job advertised with the Education Authority, but it was at a Teacher Training College, which was two grades higher than I was on, and closer to home. I applied for it, and was successful. The salary was almost £850 a year, which almost compensated for the loss of Judi's wage of £7 a week.

It was quite a small Teacher Training College where I worked in Sunderland. It was specifically for the training of the teaching of science subjects. All the 'pupils' were mature students, some as old as fifty! The only things taught there were Physics, Biology, and Chemistry. Again, I was the only lab technician, so I did everything the three lecturers requested. There was, of course, the routine setting up of experiments, looking after the animals, stock control of all the chemicals used, ordering of consumables, and ordering of various text and reference books, and lots of clearing up!

As all the students were adults, it made my life a lot easier, and there was always someone to chat to when it was quiet. I also got on very well with the lecturers, in particular the lecturer in charge, who taught physics. He realised that my interest in his subject was more than he expected from a laboratory technician, and consequently, if he was busy with administrative tasks, he would ask me to take his class for him! It added a bit more interest for me.

When Antony was about one year old, and I'd had a salary increase to just over £900, we decided to get on the housing ladder. It was too easy to buy a house and get a mortgage in 1968! We had no problem getting a 100% mortgage on the two up, two down, old terraced cottage, quite close to where we rented. The house cost us £1,850.

The monthly repayments seemed a lot of money at the time,

being about £16 a month. When I got paid, I gave Judi the weekly housekeeping, and the money for the mortgage, which was the vast majority of my salary. Judi would go down to the Building Society once a month to pay the mortgage. I had to run my motorbike, and pay the gas, electric, and rates (Council Tax) out of what I had left. Money was very tight indeed. We had been living in our new house for about ten months when, one Saturday morning a letter from the Building Society landed on the mat. It was printed in red. Always a bad sign. I only ever saw the mail on a Saturday, as I was at work when it arrived during the rest of the week.

Judi snatched the letter from me,

> "It's for me", she said, nervously.

> "It's from the Building Society", I said, "It's for both of us!".

> "Nothing to worry about", said Judi.

> "I want to read it", I snapped at her.

We read it together. It was a mortgage foreclosure notice. We had not paid the last four mortgage payments, and we had ignored the previous three letters, and this was to tell us the property was being reclaimed immediately by the Building Society. We owed them £64.

Their threat was real, harsh, and immediate. The bailiffs arrived two hours later. There were three of them. I wouldn't let them in, but they just smashed the door in, breaking the lock.

They took all of our furniture, piled it up in the street, changed the door locks, and boarded the front door up.

Judi was sitting on the sofa in the middle of the street with Antony in her arms, crying uncontrollably, saying,

> "It's all my fault. It's all my fault. I spent the money on things for Antony".

Of course, it wasn't her fault, it was mine. We were trying to live beyond our means, and I was not giving Judi enough money for the essentials we needed, simply because I didn't have it. Her only failing was burying her head in the sand and keeping everything from me.

I left Judi sitting in the street with Antony and all our furniture, and drove round to my parents' house to get my dad. I explained things very briefly, and we went back to Judi in my dad's van. We loaded all our belongings (there weren't that many) into Dad's big, old, Bedford van and went back to my parents' house, where we remained for about eight months.

We rented my parents' front room, which we lived and slept in, and shared their kitchen. It was not a good time, as Judi and my mother did not get on at all, but I couldn't afford much rent. We used to try and use the kitchen when my mother wasn't there. My mother was fine with Antony, as was my sister. My Dad was really in his element, and absolutely loved Antony living in his house, where he could see him every day.

During our stay at my parents' house, I was working very long and hard to save some money to be able to move. Apart from my full-time job, I had three additional jobs. I was a 'Bouncer' in a nightclub on Friday and Saturday nights; I had Football Pools rounds on Wednesday and Thursday evenings; was a barman at a Working Men's Club on a Sunday lunchtime; and worked overtime for my day job on Tuesday evenings.

I also took a job working in a soft drink manufacturing plant as a labourer for my three weeks annual holiday from my day job. Hard, manual work stacking crates of soft drinks all day, but it actually paid more per hour than my normal job.

Barman in the Working Men's Club was by far the easiest job. It was always busy on a Sunday lunchtime, the majority of customers, about 95% who were male, were pleasant. Several had too much to drink, but ushering them out was someone else's job. As I am pretty quick and accurate with mental arithmetic, I never felt under stress, as some of the other bar staff were. I was asked if I would like a full-time job there, but I considered it a dead-end job, so refused. I was paid about £1.50p for four hours.

My Football Pools rounds were on a commission only basis. I was paid 10% of what I collected, which was about £2 commission from each round. My rounds were in one of the roughest parts of town, and I got a lot of abuse from people who had lost the previous week. As if I could do anything about it! I was often threatened and I was actually robbed once.

Although I was quite a big lad, when two youths approached me, I was worried.

> "Give me the money", said one of the two lads standing in front of me. I thought to myself, 'I think I can manage these two.' Then from behind me, "We mean now, or you are going to get hurt".

No way I could take on three of them. I handed over my takings for the night. I was at the end of my round, obviously they knew that, so I had about £20.

They ran off without touching me, but I was quite shocked. Nothing like this had ever happened to me before.

When I went back to my Main Collectors house to report this. He reported it to the police, but this was only so he could claim the money on his insurance policy, which did not cover my commission, so I lost out on that!

From then onwards, I took to carrying a walking stick round with me.

My third part-time job was as a Bouncer in a nightclub in Sunderland. This was by far the most interesting, and by far the best rewarded. I was paid £4 each night for working from 9pm until 2am. The only problem was that I had to buy a Dinner Suit and bow tie for work. That was a £2 expenditure at the second-hand clothes shop!

There was a strict no drinking policy for staff, and if caught, it was dismissal. The three Bouncers always adhered to it, although several of the bar staff had a sly drink. I became quite friendly with one of the girls behind the bar, and as she lived quite close to me, I would give her a lift home after work. For this, she accumulated the drinks she was bought during the evening, and we shared them after we finished work, before going home.

Part of my evening was spent at the door, vetting people for correct attire (a tie!), and the ability to stand up without falling over due to being drunk!

The rest of the time was just mingling with guests, and checking there were no trouble makers, or people getting too drunk. One of the most frequent problems was drink stealers. Normally young guys who just walked around and stole the drinks of anyone who wasn't looking, or up dancing. If you caught one, it was your job to escort them off the premises, and inform them not to come back.

The main entrance to the Club was a discreet doorway, off a walkway which went over the top of the car park which was under the nightclub.

One evening I caught a drink stealer. He was particularly loud and offensive, but that wasn't that unusual.

I walked him up to the front door, as he constantly swore at me, opened the door to let him out, and then .... he pulled a knife from his pocket! I was so surprised when he lunged at me, I was caught off guard. I felt a pain. He had knifed me in my left side, just below my ribs, and I was bleeding heavily.

I became angry and lost my temper. Rushing toward him, I pushed him through the door and against the rail on the walkway. He shouted at me,

"You can't touch me here. I'm not in the Club!".

Technically, he was correct, but I'd lost my temper.

"F*** that!", I said.

Blood was oozing from my side and running down my shirt and trousers as I picked him up and threw him over the rail onto the cars in the car park, about six feet below. I then fainted.

The police and ambulance were called. We both went to the hospital. I had a few stitches and was sent home. My assailant had a broken shoulder and wrist, cracked ribs, and a cut to his head. He stayed in hospital for observation for several days.

The outcome was that I was charged with 'common assault', and sent a summons to appear in Court several months later. I wrote to the Court and, eventually, With the backing of the nightclub, the case was dropped, but I was given a written warning!

My side had healed in a couple of weeks, and I've no idea what happened to my assailant. Nor do I care.

Probably my fourth close call in life's game of chance!

I was now a qualified "Industrial Measurement & Control" technician. Not that I seemed to need these skills in the work I was doing. It was early 1969, we had been living in that one room in my parents' house for about eight months, and I was getting a bit fed-up with things. I was starting to think about my future.

Was I going to be a laboratory assistant for the next forty years?

It didn't appeal to me!

What should I do?

I read a lot of technical journals and magazines, and I had read about some electronic calculating machines, which were going to be the thing of the future. They were called 'computers', and they needed people to work them. Operators and programmers.

Deciding that this was an avenue worth investigating, I soon found out that there were only two companies who were making or operating computers. One was called IBM, the other was ICL.

I decided to write to both and ask if they had any trainee positions available for reasonably educated, but unskilled personnel.

I drew up my CV and sent it to both of these companies. Within a week, ICL responded saying they had nothing suitable for me. I was a little disheartened, as this was the first time I'd applied for a job and not got an interview.

The following week IBM responded, and asked if I would like to pop into their Personnel Department in Newcastle, in two weeks' time, for a chat. They did say that there were no vacancies at the moment, but I might be considered in the future.

It was one foot in the door! That's all I could hope for at this stage. I spent the next two weeks learning everything there was to know about IBM as a company, and anything I could find on the subject of computers.

The day of the interview came round, and I turned up at the new IBM four story office block in Newcastle.

I was given a temporary pass by Security at the main entrance, and led up two flights to the Personnel Department.

I was surprised that three people were present for our 'chat', but never mind. Eric was the Operations Manager, and the other two were from Personnel. They asked me about what I did, and my aspirations for the future. I told them, emphasizing that my knowledge of computers was minimal. They did ask if I knew anything about IBM, as they were going to tell me some background to the company. They were surprised that I knew IBMs origins went back to tabulating machines in the 1880s, and IBM was founded in 1924 when it started making electric typewriters, and they currently had a 1401 series computer, which was soon to be replaced by the new 360 series.

I also told them that I knew computers worked using only binary arithmetic and register to register transfer based on Octal or Hexadecimal numbering systems, but I didn't know how!

They seemed impressed, and said they may have a trainee roll available in about six months' time, for which I would be considered. That seemed like a lifetime away to me, so I left, thinking I'd never hear from them again.

The following week, on a Saturday morning, I was quite surprised when there was a knock on the front door. My mother and father didn't hear it, so I answered. We never had visitors!

Standing on the doorstep was Eric!

Caught a little by surprise, I wasn't too sure why he was there.

"Come on in", I blurted out.

"Sorry about the state of the place", I added, as I shuffled things around to free up one of the two chairs we had. I was a little embarrassed having a stranger see the one room in which we lived. Luckily, Judi was out with Antony, so we could both have a seat.

"We are living here temporarily while we save up for a house", I said, trying to hide my embarrassment.

"Good for You!", said Eric. "It was the same when I got married".

"I'm not here to see where you live", Eric continued. "I want to offer you a job, but it's very much below your skill level. It's the only vacancy we have, and it's available immediately, but we always promote from within, so you should be able to progress at the speed you are capable of."

"What is the job?" was my response.

"Assistant in the paper store", was the reply. "You will be unloading printer paper from the vans it arrives at the Data Centre in, taking it to the paper store, and then into the Computer Room when the Computer Operator asks you to."

Not the sort of job I had envisaged, working for the biggest computer company in the World!

"We start none University degree staff at the bottom, and see how things work out", Eric continued. "We will start you on the salary you are earning now, for a three-month probationary period, then we will do a review to see what happens next. If you want the job, there will be an offer letter in the post on Monday."

We talked for about half an hour, as I obviously didn't want to work in a paper store for the rest of eternity! Opportunities were available for those who are willing to work for them, and this was a very new industry in 1969.

Eric duly left, and an hour later Judi returned home. We discussed the offer. Judi was concerned that I would be leaving a relatively good job to work as a 'storeman', as she put it. But I wanted to change my career path and saw this as an opportunity to do this, and there was no reduction in my salary and no obvious salary scale ceiling, as there was with the Education Authority job I had.

We agreed I would hand in my notice, as soon as I received the IBM offer letter.

I accepted the IBM offer. It is fifteen miles from Sunderland to Newcastle, and took about 40 minutes to drive there. I had made my mind up that we were going to have our own house before I started IBM a month later. Also, that I would have a car when my IBM probationary period had finished, as I was expecting to get a reasonable increase in salary because I would ensure I'd do the job well!

Always a man of my word, we started looking for an inexpensive house.

My approach to buying a property had changed since the distressing incident of the previous year, and I decided I would not get into too much debt, and I was thinking twice about using a Building Society for a twenty-five-year loan. It seemed to me that if I got into financial difficulty when a Building Society is involved, the outcome is likely to be disastrous for me, again. I'd had an experience I definitely did not want to repeat!

We were looking for a house similar to the one we had repossessed, in the same general area. Everything was way out of our price range, as I wanted to buy the house with a five-year bank loan if possible. The going rate was around the £2,000 mark. I did manage to find a 'fixer-upper' cottage, which was two up, two down, as we wanted, but it had a dampness problem, and had been empty for five years. It was within our price range, being only £700!

Because of its condition no Building Society would give a loan on it, and the seller wanted a £100 deposit, which we had.

We bought it! £100 deposit, and a £600 loan from the seller. We agreed an interest rate of about 12%, and repayments over three years at £20 a month.

Unfortunately, the house had never been modernised, and the condition was very bad. Most of the ground floor did not have a floor, because there had been a water leak for five years, and it had rotted away. The only water supply was a cold tap in the small kitchen. There was no bathroom, and the toilet was at the bottom of the yard.

Aunt Lottie was still keeping touch. She would come to see Antony almost every week. When we told her we were going to buy another house, the first thing she said was,

"I could come and live with you, and help look after Antony."

Not actually something Judi and I had thought about, but Judi wanted to go back to work on a part time basis, so this could be a good idea. Aunt Lottie wasn't getting on too well with the friend she was living with, she later told us.

I managed to get our 'new' house into a liveable state in about three weeks, by giving up my Football Pools rounds and Sunday lunchtime barman job, and working on the house until about midnight every day, and during the day on weekends. Dick helped me when he could.

Many of the floor beams needed replacing, together with much of the flooring. The electrics needed redoing, but I had a friend who was an electrician. With the aid of a few trade books, I managed to sort out the plumbing, and even installed central heating downstairs with a second-hand boiler I found in a scrap yard! I even put in an 'over sink' water heater, so at least we didn't have to boil a kettle every time we wanted some hot water.

Judi and Dick both helped with decorating, and within a month it looked pretty good.

Just to make sure I didn't get into any problems paying the £20 a month house repayment, I used a new-fangled payment system which had just started in the bank. It was called 'direct debit'. It was complex and time taking to set-up, but at least I didn't have to worry about missing any payments, as long as my bank balance was in credit!

Although I was really glad to get away from living in that one room in my parents' house, I was grateful to them. Apart from giving us a very cheap roof over our heads, my dad had taught me to drive a car. He had never taken a driver's test, in fact, I don't think he even had a Driver's License! I booked my driving test, and he gave me three lessons in the week before I took it.

The fact that he had not taken a driving test became obvious when I took my test. I failed, but as I was told on which things I had failed, I could correct them. I read a book about learning to drive, and had another six lessons with my dad, but this time I ignored everything he said, and he was just my passenger! I passed my test on the second attempt.

We moved into our house about two weeks after I started with IBM. The Education Authority paid me monthly in arrears, IBM did the same, but actually it was only three weeks in arrears as pay day was the 20th of the month, and I had some holiday pay to come, so we had money to buy things for the house.

After about four weeks, Aunt Lottie moved in, and Judi got a job as a typist with a mail order catalogue company based in Sunderland.

It was only one month after starting with IBM that I was offered a job as a Production Control Clerk. This involved setting up the Job Control Language (JCL) input for the computer to process. It was initially quite daunting, as it involved setting up programmes with paper tape or card data input, ensuring the correct disks were mounted on the computer drives, selecting the correct input master tape and intermediate working tapes, and ensuring the correct dates were changed on the date cards. In many cases the input data cards had to be sorted by the Production Control Clerk on a sorting machine. There were often a lot of data cards, some jobs having up to 20,000 cards. The correct paper had to be requested from the paper store, but I knew all about that!

All of the jobs for overnight had to be set up before leaving at 5pm, so sometimes this could be nearer 6pm. I enjoyed it! At last, at twenty-four years of age, I'd found a career in an industry I really wanted to be in.

My salary, after one month in my new role, was increased from £900 to £1,100. I was able to give up my part time jobs, and actually spend evenings at home with Judi and Antony.

I bought our first four wheeled car at about this time. It was a 1953 'sit up and beg' Ford Popular 103E. I found it in a back street near me. Looked like it hadn't been used for a long while. It had flat tyres, no windscreen wipers, and the bodywork was rusty. I knocked on the back door of the house it was parked outside of.

A scruffy looking middle-aged guy in a grey (used to be white) vest opened it.

"Wadda yu want", he grunted.

"How much for the car?", I said, "and what's wrong with it?"

"£20. There's no radiator or MOT." he responded.

"It also needs at least one tyre and the wipers are missing. I'll give you a fiver", I replied.

We haggled for five minutes, and I paid him £7 for the car.

Went down the scrap yard on Saturday morning, bought the bits I needed for £5. Sorted it out on Sunday, including painting it by hand with a tin of 'Valspar' black paint. Took it for its MOT on Monday, and it was on the road on Tuesday.

We did have a few good weekend trips with it.

We went to the Lake District one weekend. It was about 100 miles each way, and the weather was terrible. The car had vacuum wipers, which meant the faster the car went, the slower the wipers went. Bloody terrible system. The engine was a bit clapped out, and it had only a three-speed gearbox (and second gear didn't engage), and one of the hills we went up was too steep for bottom gear, so I had to reverse up.

It lasted three months before the engine blew up. I drove it to the scrap yard and he gave me £10 for it, so it was cheap motoring for three months!

I went a bit up-market with my next car, which was a 1957 Ford Anglia 100E. It was more 'car shaped' than my previous Ford, but still had the three-speed gearbox and a gear lever the length of an umbrella handle!

£25 was paid for this twelve year old car, with 80,000 miles on the clock. It was fine as a family car, but drove like a jelly! I didn't like it much, and only had it for two months, before selling it for £30.

I replaced my Anglia with a Volkswagen Beetle. I heard how reliable they were, and my old Fords didn't like starting in the cold or the wet. The Beetle was air cooled and had a reputation for starting every time, no matter what the weather was like. The disadvantage was the six-volt electric system, which meant the headlights were like candles. It did have a four-speed gearbox as well. VW Beetles held their price well, and I was surprised to find a 1959 one for sale privately for £90. I went to see it, and liked it. It had a funny roller type thing for the accelerator, but seemed to have loads of storage space with the boot at the front and room for two suitcases behind the rear seats. The engine sounded like a sack of hammers, which was normal. I fell in love with it immediately, but the mileage seemed a bit high to me.

"What's the mileage?", I said, sticking my head through the window to try and read the odometer. "I can't quite make it out."

"The clock is reading 72,000 miles", the seller replied.

"A little high", was my response.

"That's nothing for one of these", he retorted, "and it's only the second time round!"

I gave a visible gasp!

"What! It's done 172,000 miles!" I spluttered.

> "That's why it's only £90 and not £180", the Seller explained. "These engines are good for at least 250,000, before they need any major attention."

I told him I'd think about it and get back to him the following day. I spent the rest of the day in the public library, reading about Volkswagen Beetles! I was impressed with what I read, and went back the next day and bought the car.

It was about this time I decided I would like to join the Territorial Army (TA) and become a part-time soldier. I had just missed conscription by a couple of years, so I never did any National Service. Often thought I would like to have tried it.

The main drawback for me was that I had to shave off my beard! I'd had it since I left school, and now in my 70's, I still have it.

The commitment was something I thought I could fit in with my lifestyle. I joined the Sunderland 251 Field Ambulance. It was one evening a week attendance, with a minimum of, I think, twenty weeks a year; six week-end camps a year; and an annual two-week Training Camp. I wasn't very keen on the evening sessions, which seemed to have a lot of marching and rifle cleaning, but not much First Aid or driving.

My main duty was as a driver. The week-ends were something different though! Out on the moors driving Land Rover ambulances, or the 1940's four-ton Commer trucks, which the Army called three-ton trucks so we could drive them on our car driving licences. Although I wasn't a driving veteran, my driving skills were pretty good, and I quickly learned how to reverse a Commer truck and trailer (normally a gun carriage) very efficiently, and soon mastered the 'crash' gearboxes!

One day on manoeuvres, I was given a brand-new Land Rover Ambulance to drive. We were simulating emergency evacuation of soldiers from the front lines, and we were told to not waste any time getting them back to the Field Hospital. Taking my Sergeant at his word, I was driving very quickly across the moor, which was our 'no man's land', and hit a deep ravine. The vehicle stood almost on its nose, and there was a loud cracking noise. The chassis had broken in half. A write-off with 200 miles on the clock! I was not popular, and had to peel an awful lot of potatoes!

The field exercises, driving, and the obstacle courses were great fun, but I didn't like marching. I wasn't a good soldier, and was always in trouble for smiling! I did it because I thought it was fun, and I got paid. For the two-week camp I actually got paid twice, since IBM also paid my salary, and gave me the two weeks off without loss of holiday entitlement.

I was with the TA for about two years.

With the reported reliability of my 'new' car, and as we had a bit of money to spare, (Judi was also working and Aunt Lottie was living with us and looking after Antony), we decided to have a camping holiday in the summer of 1970.

I bought a second hand two-bedroom tent, loads of camping bits and pieces, and a small five foot by three foot trailer to carry it around in. That left plenty of room in the car. We had just got a Golden Labrador, who we called Donna, and she shared the rear seat with Antony, who was now three and a half.

We went to the Norfolk Broads. A bit ambitious, as it was about 300 miles each way, but I was confident in my little grey Beetle. My confidence was well founded. Not a single problem for the whole week, apart from Antony complaining Donna had more than her fair share of the back seat!

"Mam, Donna's got all the seat!", moaned Antony.

"Push her back over her side", responded Judi.

"She's too heavy to move", was Antony's response.

Donna said nothing, she just stretched out and snored!

We had our tent pitched on a Camping Site, and would travel

around the area during the day, returning to the tent for an evening meal.

Often, we would stop at a pub for a drink on the way back to the camping site. Children were not allowed in pubs then, so we left Donna looking after Antony in the back of the car for an hour. Before we went in Antony was given a glass of lemonade, a bag of crisps, and a chocolate flake. Donna was happy with just a bag of crisps. Normally they were both asleep when we returned, but it was Antony lying on Donna this time!

On one of our days out we hired a small motorboat for the day, and cruised up and down the Broads. At lunchtime we stopped at a riverside pub, where they allowed children to come into the garden area, as long as we had a meal there. Dogs were also allowed. We had a couple of drinks and a meal, with Antony and Donna quite happily playing on the grass. We stayed about three hours, before returning to where we had tied up our boat.

It was a shock, but at the same time very funny.

The boat was still tied to the mooring bollard, but the water level had dropped about three feet. The boat was hanging, pointed end up, with the back dangling in the water. I hadn't left any slack when I tied it up, and the canal water level had dropped!

To everyone's amusement, I had to untie the boat and let it drop into the water. I then clambered down into it, told Antony to jump, and I caught him; then got Judi to push Donna over the edge so I could catch her, and finally got Judi to dangle over the quay, and helped her aboard.

Rounds of applause from the onlookers as I rather embarrassedly set off the mile or so down the canal to return the boat.

I did my job as a Production Control Clerk for about a year before I was offered a position as a Computer Operator, which was really what I wanted to do. This was shift work, but not a problem for me, as I had been used to working shifts at the Paper Mill. As a

Trainee, I was on shift with a Senior Operator for the first three months. It was the same guy, Alan, all of the time. There were normally two operators on the day and evening shifts, but it was by yourself for the night shift. The night shift was always the quietest, as that was when the big overnight jobs were run. Alan was very happy to have company on the night shift for my first three months as a Trainee.

The Computer Room was huge!

The computer consisted of a Central Processing Unit (CPU), six ten plate disc drives, ten magnetic tape units, a paper tape reader, a card reader, a card punch, two high speed fanfold paper printers, and the operator's console. The console was next to the CPU. The CPU footprint was about six feet by four feet and stood about five feet high, and held the 64 Kilobit of core memory. (The 'brain' of the computer.) Core memory was physically 64 x 1,024 (65,536) small iron rings, with a single wire passing through each ring.

Just to put things in perspective, my current mobile phone has 64GB of memory in it, which is exactly one million times more powerful than the 360/30 computer!

The room was air conditioned, which kept the computer cool, and the computer operator cold!

When I started as a computer operator, the Data Centre had just taken delivery of a new IBM 360/30, which had replaced the old IBM 1401 model. The new 360 was far more powerful, but many of the old programs were written for the 1401, which meant a lot of the time the 360 was running in 1401 emulation mode. This meant a lot more work for the operator, who had umpteen switches to set on the CPU front panel, and much more interaction through the console.

One thing IBM was really keen on was education. Apart from the basic courses offered for whatever job you did; they had a massive library of IBM self-teach technical books. When on night shift alone, when some of the very large processing jobs were running, I had an hour or two most nights to study these books, which I did avidly.

I progressed through the grades quite quickly, and within two years I was a Shift Leader. Not too many people to lead as there were only two of us on a shift. But it did show that my competency was increasing, along with my salary.

Some nights, when on night shift, I brought Donna into work with me. She liked night shifts, as she loved just sniffing around the computer room, or napping on the floor, and she loved spending all day in bed with me!

One night shift, somewhere around 3am, Donna became very restless. This was not like her. She normally had a pee before we came to the office, but I thought she must want to go out. I took her downstairs and out through Reception and into the street. She just sniffed about a little, then wanted to go back in. We went back in, I had a five minute chat with Bill, the Security Guard, who was the only other person in the building, then went back upstairs to the Computer Suite.

Donna still didn't settle. She was restless and wanted to go out again. I started running a large processing job which wouldn't require any operator intervention for 20 minutes and opened the computer room door to see what she wanted. She headed for the stairwell, so I assumed she must want to go out again. To my surprise, she started going upstairs, towards the Programmers offices.

At the top of the stairs there was a locked door. There was one on each floor, and they were locked for fire and security reasons every night. Only the Security Guard had a key. Donna sniffed at the door, and I could hear a slight rustling from inside. I was feeling a little scared now! Someone must have broken in and was searching for valuables.

I quickly returned to the stairwell and rushed down the stairs to alert Bill. Bill was sitting with his feet up on his desk in Reception, reading his newspaper. It was almost 4am by now.

I told him what I had heard, and he said he had checked that floor about an hour previously and that I must be mistaken. Perhaps it was an air conditioning unit on the blink, or someone had left a fan switched on.

There was absolutely no way anyone could be in there! All the windows were sealed, as the building was air conditioned. The rear door was locked, and no one had come in the front door. The closed circuit security system showed no activity whatsoever, other than Donna and I going up the stairs to the second floor.

I was insistent that he did his next round early. Begrudgingly, he agreed.

Together we walked up the stairs to the second floor. We reached the locked wooden double doors, stopped and listed.

"Can't hear a thing.", Bill said.

"Neither can I, now!", I agreed.

"You must have been hearing things", was Bills response, "but I'll open up anyway, just to make sure everything is okay".

Everything was certainly NOT okay!

It looked like a hurricane had passed through the room There were about twenty desks where the Programmers sat, but none of the desks was a tidy looking work area. There was computer fan-fold paper littered about like Christmas streamers, writing paper was strewn all over the floor, along with punch cards, paper tape, pens, rubber bands and personal knick-knacks from the workers desks. Most of the chairs were on their sides, and several desks were upturned.

"Vandals!", I said.

"But how did they get in?", questioned Bill.

Bill checked all of the windows. All were still tightly sealed. He checked the rear door, which was also still locked. We went downstairs to the security area, and Bill went through all of the security tapes for the night. Absolutely nothing on them, other than my walk up the stairs.

Bill phoned in the incident to his Head Office, and a senior member of the Security Company arrived within half an hour. I couldn't get involved any further, as I had jobs to run, and this would not be a good excuse to not get a company's payroll out on time.

As there were no signs of any forced entry, and nothing was stolen, the incident was never reported to the police. Most of the mess was tidied up before 9am, when the office workers came in. Very few people were aware of the incident, and no explanation was ever given.

I did a little research myself, and found out that, before its demolition, a large house used to stand on the site where the IBM building had been built. I was told, and I think I must now believe it, that the occupant of that house had murdered his wife in an upstairs bedroom. I know most readers will not believe this, but the only explanation I can give is that the building is haunted!!

My drive to work from Sunderland to Newcastle was about fifteen miles. About five miles outside of Newcastle was a very fast dual carriageway, known locally as the Felling bypass.

One day on my way home from work I was driving along the Felling bypass. It had been raining, and the roads were wet and greasy. This was sometime in 1972 and I was still driving my VW Beetle.

It was about 4:30pm and traffic was heavy. I was driving behind a large truck carrying one of the containers used on container ships. His brake lights went on, but not a problem as there was plenty of space between us, even though the road was wet and slippery. I came to a halt about six feet from him.

"That was a close one", I thought.

A second or two later there was a deafening bang from behind me, and was being pushed toward the looming container in front of me. It seemed to happen in slow motion, but was only an instant. I ducked down as I was pushed into the container lorry. I could see the underside of the lorry as the windscreen and front pillars of my car were pushed back. At the same time, I could feel something pushing into the back of my seat. It was the back seat.

It seems that the container truck in front of me had braked suddenly and unexpectedly, because a pedestrian crossed the road, rather than use the pedestrian bridge!

The large wagon following me was caught unaware, and was late braking. As a result, I was crushed between the two vehicles like a grape in a vice.

Miraculously, I was totally unscathed.

My fifth brush with death!

My car was a total write off, for which I received £50 from my Insurer. The driver of the lorry that hit me was prosecuted for driving 'without due care and attention'.

Shortly after my road accident we decided to move house. We had finished paying for our cottage, and had improved it a lot, including having a bathroom built onto the side of the kitchen. We had spent well over £1,000 on improvements on our £600 house, but house prices were starting to go up quickly, and our house was now worth more than £4.000.

We decided to move to Peterlee, which was a 'new town', for two reasons. Firstly, new houses were being sold at a huge discount to get people to move there, and secondly, Judi's Aunt Mary and Uncle Stan lived there. Also, Great Aunt Lottie had decided she didn't want to live with us any longer and had moved in with one of her friends who attended the same church. (Unlike Judi and myself, Aunt Lottie was very religious.) Judi had stopped going out to work, and was being a full-time mother.

We found a house in Peterlee which we really liked. It was a three bedroom, through lounge, with a garden and a garage. It was right on the edge of the Estate, overlooking a wooded area with walks through it. It was a concrete slab design, with a flat roof. A very modern concept in 1973!

It was only £4,600, and our small terraced cottage in Sunderland sold for £4,200.

The problem for me was the commute. It was ten miles further to work for me, but IBM gave me a small salary increase as compensation. IBM also had a Scientific Centre in Peterlee, which had a specialised 'number crunching' computer used for scientific research. They only had a part-time computer operator, so I agreed to work there for one day a week. It was boring, as all the jobs involved a vast amount of computer processing with very little operator intervention.

We both quite liked Peterlee, and Judi spent a lot of time with her Aunt Mary, and we often joined them in their caravan at weekends in the countryside.

I replaced my written off VW Beetle with a brand new yellow VW 1,300 Beetle! This was the first new car I had ever owned. I absolutely loved it! As my commute to work was over fifty miles a day, I thought a new car would be super reliable, and it was. It was also great for towing around our little camping trailer, and I actually kept this car for two years. I only sold it because it had done 35,000 miles, and I was offered £900 for it. I only paid £1,050 for it when I bought it new.

I had also become interested in customising cars, so I also bought a ten-year-old Beetle which I customised. I replaced the underpowered engine with a Porsche engine, fitted lowered uprated suspension, flared the wheel arches to accommodate the ten inch wide front, and twelve inch wide rear racing tyres, replaced the bus sized steering wheel with a small sports one, and fitted custom seats to both the front and back. I also painted it pink, and painted the chrome black. After two days, I also replaced the VW clutch with a Porsche one, as I burned it out!

It was an eye catcher, and was very fast for its day. I surprised many cars on the motorway as I flashed by at 110mph! I called her the Pink Panther.

One day, it was stolen from Altrincham town centre while we were shopping. I reported it to the police, who said it shouldn't be too difficult to spot, and suggested I try driving around looking for it. Stupid idea I thought. However, I did find my Pink Panther about four hours later, just parked by the side of the road only about a mile from where it was taken. It was on the reserve petrol tank, but not damaged in any way. On the seat was a note which read 'I've had a great drive. Doesn't it go fast?'

Someone had obviously taken it for a 'Joyride'!

It was at about this time that something even newer was happening in the Data Processing World. It was called Data Communications. Up to this point, all data was brought to the computer in either paper form, which was converted to punch cards, or as paper tape, which was normally automatically produced by another machine. Data Comms allowed the data to be received directly from a remote location.

I became very interested in this as IBM in Newcastle started receiving data directly from the Harland & Wolff shipyard in Belfast. The data transfer was very slow, at only 134bps (bits per second), and it took several hours for this data to be transmitted down a telephone line.

There was no obvious career progression for me at IBM in Newcastle. My next step could have been my boss, but that was unlikely for many years, and IBM Newcastle was quite a small Data Centre.

I was asked if I would consider moving to the IBM Data Centre in Manchester, as a Shift Leader. There were six or seven operators on each shift in Manchester as they had four computers, and each ran a different Operating System. Judi and I talked about it, and Antony was only seven years old, so we thought it would not disrupt his schooling too much.

The prices of houses in the North-West were a lot more than in the North-East, even though they seemed to be rising fast in the North-East. We had lived in Peterlee for less than two years, and our house was now worth £7,000, but an affordable three-bedroom semi-detached house in an inexpensive area, five miles from where I was going to work, was £7,500.

Judi and I quite liked our time in the North-West. We made many new friends, as did Antony, but I never really took to my new job. Shift leader in a Data Centre the size of Manchester was more a management position, and I was only expected to operate the computers if we were short of staff, which was infrequently. I was more interested in Data Communications, which was getting more sophisticated. I continued to learn, even learning to read 'System Dumps', which was how Data Comms problems were investigated.

I started to get a little bored with the Shift Leader job, but I realised that no one seemed to know anything about the Data Comms. I suggested that we needed a single point of contact for this, and was given the job of Data Comms Specialist, although I was definitely not a specialist! However, I did know which manuals to consult to find out things, and which technical person knew about the different elements involved. My work suddenly became interesting again, at least for a while.

A few of the guys at work decided we should do something to help out a local charity. It started out as four of us, but ended up with just Derick and I, who decided we would do a sponsored parachute jump! We sorted out some sponsors, and arranged for the event to happen one sunny Saturday.

The event took place at a small airport near Manchester, which had a flying club and a parachute club.

There were two of us who decided to do the jump. We had about two hours classroom tuition, followed by two hours practical tuition. The classroom tuition was basically explaining how you get out of the plane when it's flying so fast, about wind speed, how a parachute works, and lots of safety stuff, including how to pack your own parachute. Packing your own parachute was a bit worrying, but we were very well supervised doing this! The practical training involved jumping off an eight-foot wall into gravel to learn how to land.

The training was over, so we packed our parachutes, and walked over to the aeroplane.

> "What the Hell is this?", said my jumping partner, Derick.

> "It doesn't have a door!", I exclaimed.

> "You cannot jump out of a four-seater plane with the door still on", the instructor explained, "Remember we were talking about how fast you will be travelling? We wouldn't be able to open the door", he continued.

> "Going to be bloody draughty!", I said.

We clambered into the small plane. The instructor and Derick in the back, and me kneeling beside the pilot in the front, as the front seat and the door had both been removed.

We took off.

It was bloody windy!

We climbed up to the jump height, I've no idea how high we were, and the instructor said,

> "You're out first, Jeff", as he secured my rip cord to an anchor point on the floor. As this was my first jump it was a 'static line jump', which meant I didn't have to pull my ripcord. The parachute would deploy when I was about twenty feet below the plane.

I was a little apprehensive, to say the least.

We had slowed down to about 60mph so I could get out of the plane.

> "Off you go!", screamed the instructor over the noise of the wind, "Just step out onto the wheel and grab hold of the wing strut, like we practised on the ground, then just push yourself off backwards."

This was nothing like what we practised on the ground!

I forced myself through the door opening, struggling against the wind, which I was convinced was blowing at over 200mph!

I cautiously stepped onto the wheel, and to my, and everyone else's surprise, the wheel started to spin. Out of the corner of my eye I Could see the pilot yanking feverishly at a lever on the floor.

The wheel continued to spin. I was like a hamster in a wheel.

I couldn't grab the wing strut securely and just tumbled off the wheel, totally out of control, and fell head first. I felt the jerk as the ripcord tightened, then the parachute opened. I was upside down with my foot caught in the ropes of the parachute, which were all twisted. I looked up and the parachute looked like a number eight! Instead of one big circle above me there were two smaller ones, one a little larger than the other.

"Shit, this is it!", I thought.

"Don't panic!". I told myself, as I was falling head first to the ground below. At least I didn't seem to be falling fast, although I wasn't sure how slow or fast, I should be descending. I could see the problem. All I needed to do was untangle my foot and I should turn the right way up. After what seemed an eternity, I did manage to untangle myself, and I did turn round the right way, and I was still pretty high up. The problem now was that I had drifted away from the landing area on the airfield, and was going to land in the adjacent field which had cattle in it. I now realised that perhaps I was coming down a little faster than I should. The ground definitely seemed to be approaching faster than it did when I was jumping into the gravel during training! As I approached the ground, the cattle started running about, and as luck would have it, I landed on one!

The cow didn't seem bothered about it, but it had caused me to land badly and I hurt my back.

After a few minutes a land rover turned up to retrieve me.

My back hurt for days, but I had a good yarn to spin in the pub that evening!

Derick didn't do his jump!

I never found out what the problem had been with the aeroplane wheel. I was just given a fuzzy explanation about a problem with the brake cable.

An inverted, or blown periphery was the experience the instructor told me I had undergone, and it was an extremely rare occurrence. Not something I would recommend!

I think I would call this my sixth brush with mortality.

By now I had changed my car again. I sold the yellow Beetle because the mileage was increasing on it too fast, and I was offered a good price for it. I also sold the Pink Panther to another Beetle enthusiast. A red Ford Cortina Mark IV, 2,000 GT, which I bought cheap from one of the IBM Salesmen, was our next car.

I also customised a black Ford Capri 3,000GT, just as a hobby project.

I had always liked 'fixing things', or at least, trying to. In the shed I had a box full of cogs and springs from failed watch repair projects. I always seemed to have some bits left after I had reassembled the watch. Funnily enough, none of the watches I repaired ever worked again!

One day Antony came to me.

> "My Action Man is broken" he said presenting me with a head and torso, two legs, and two arms.
>
> "I'll soon fix that for you, Ant. It should only take half an hour." I promised.

It wasn't as easy as it first looked. It was basically held together by a thick rubber band which held the arms and legs on, but the hook on one of the legs had broken off. I had no problem replacing the hook on the leg, but I was really struggling to get the thing back together. The rubber band was just too strong to manoeuvre the arms and legs into place, together. After about two hours I managed it.

> "Here you go, Ant. It's fixed!" I said as I presented it back to him.
>
> "What have you done!" he exclaimed. "His legs are on the wrong way!"

In my struggle with Action Man, I had somehow got the legs mixed up, and they were on the wrong side of the torso. I managed to convince Antony that this was the only way it would go back together, and after all, he now had a unique Action Man, with a bum at the front!

Things just plodded along, and we celebrated the Queens Silver Jubilee in June 1977 with a street party we had at home. It was a great day. We put up lots of decorations, organised outdoor games, like a tug of war, three-legged races, sack races, and wheelbarrow races. Our street was a dead end, so we put up trestle tables and all of the women made food, which we ate outside with lashings on beer. Probably a little different to how the Queen spent her day!

Antony was ten years old in early 1977. He attended the local school, and supported Manchester United football team. I had never been interested in football, so I was glad when one of his friends who lived only a few doors away was a supporter also.

Judi had got fed up being a housewife, and took on a part-time typist's job at the Shell refinery, which was about five miles away. The working hours fitted in nicely with Antony's school hours.

Dick, who now worked in Bedford, used to come and visit us for the week-end about once a month. Always a bit of a boozy time, and always culminating in a late-night Indian curry after pub closing time on a Saturday.

I very seldom saw my other long time friend, Barry, who was best man at my wedding. He got his degree at Liverpool University, got a job there, and has never left. He was there until his retirement.

On the other hand, I was getting a bit restless again! I'd been the 'Data Comms Specialist' for a couple of years, but nothing really exciting seemed to happen. There were problems, but they were always similar to previous problems, so became a little boring.

It was also a time of very high inflation, and Government restrictions on salary increases. Salary increases were limited to 5% at this time, although inflation was about 16% in 1976, and 24% in the previous year! It seemed a good time to work abroad.

I decided I would like to work abroad for a while, and approached IBM about it. They said I could apply for a vacancy in Paris, which I was well qualified for, but I really wanted somewhere 'different'. I asked about India or the Middle East, but was told that would not be possible.

I went home one evening after work and Judi and I had a long talk about our future. Judi was also quite adventurous, and although by now we had been on several holidays in Europe, she was quite keen to see other more distant parts of the World, and we were concerned about the high inflation rate.

We decided I should look for a job abroad.

Chapter Three

Iran

I was looking for somewhere a bit 'different' to go and work. At that time the best place to look for any computer related work was the monthly computer magazines, which always had pages of job vacancies. For a few weeks I scanned these magazines for something I thought would be both interesting, challenging, and lucrative. There was lots of choice, but nothing that seemed that much different.

Then I found it!

A job as a Computer Operations Manager for a big shoe company in Tehran, Iran, who had just purchased an IBM computer to do all of their logistics, stock control, distribution, and payroll. Looked good to me, the only snag I could initially see, was that I was too young for the job! I was thirty-two, and the age range was thirty-five to fifty. I still applied, and was rewarded with an interview, which took place in Manchester, and was carried out by a Computer Recruitment Consultancy.

I didn't expect to get past the first interview, mainly because of my age, but also, I had never been in a management position before. I sailed through the interview, and I think the main plus point on my side, was the fact that I had been working for IBM for eight years. There was a short list of three candidates, and I was offered the job the following week, on condition I would start as soon as I had worked my one-month notice period with IBM.

I handed in my one months' notice to IBM.

"You're mad!", was my Bosses response, "Nobody ever leaves IBM. We are too good a Company!"

"I've nothing against IBM", I said, "but I want to experience a different culture and way of life."

"You're mad.", he repeated.

He went with me to see the Human Resources Manager. My Boss showed my letter of resignation to him, and told him the reason I was leaving. The HR Manager turned to me and said,

"You are totally mad!"

End of Leaving Interview!

My salary with IBM was now about £4,000. The job with the Melli Shoe Company was about £4,200 (after taxes), and I was given free family accommodation, a company car, four weeks holiday, one return home airline ticket per person per year, and local school fees paid for my son, Antony.

We decided not to sell our house, but to rent it out, so there was not a problem regarding selling the house. We also decided to rent it furnished. The main problem was our dog. Unfortunately, Donna had been run over by a car the previous year, after digging her way out of our back garden and wandering onto a nearby main road. We had quite quickly bought another dog. She was an Old English Sheepdog, who we called Beth, and was only about ten months old when we were leaving the UK. As it happened, we knew the family who had taken her sister, and they were very keen to adopt Beth.

Judi wanted to take most of our personal possessions with us, so she spent most of her time carefully wrapping two full dinner sets, three tea sets, about forty crystal glasses, and a multitude of cookery books, as well as all our clothes. Melli Shoe had arranged shipping (without charge) of anything we wanted to take, apart from my car. We were given about fifty boxes so we could do our own packing, and were told it would take about three weeks for our shipment to get from our house to Tehran. We decided to try and get everything packed two weeks before we left, so we would have our possessions sooner when we reached Iran. I also sold my car two weeks before we left, but rented one for the last two weeks.

I was given all the relevant information and the airline tickets by the recruitment company well in advance.

Everything was packed two weeks before we were ready to go, a furniture van turned up at our house, and we waved goodbye to our possessions as the van trundled down the street. We hoped to be reunited within a few weeks.

The day of our departure arrived. We were all edgy and apprehensive.

A car was sent for us, which took us to Manchester airport, from where we flew to Heathrow for an Iran Air flight. The Heathrow to Tehran flight was direct and took about seven hours. The flight was uneventful and we reached our destination on time, arriving at about 7pm.

It had been arranged for us to be collected and taken to the hotel we would be staying at until our permanent accommodation was sorted out.

The plane landed. The doors opened and we descended the aircraft steps.

> "Careful of the heat blowing out of the engine", I told Judi, "It's really hot!"

The engines were already switched off! The heat and humidity was the oppressive climate! I was struggling to breathe, and started sweating profusely. We hadn't realised the extent of the heat and humidity in Tehran in July.

Customs were not a problem. Probably because no one seemed to speak English, so we were just nodded through the Arrival Hall. We had an airport trolley with our suitcases on it, standing outside of an airport in a foreign country, where we knew no one, and it was a hot sticky evening. Men kept coming up to us and offering their services as a Taxi, at least I think so, since none spoke English. After we had stood there for ten minutes, I was beginning to think that maybe I hadn't made a good decision here! Judi was looking worried, but Antony just seemed to be loving the experience.

Then I heard a voice from behind me,

> "Jeff Covelle? Are you Jeff & Judi Covelle?", the male voice said.
>
> "And Antony", I responded.
>
> "Oh! I was told there were two to collect, but never mind", the mystery man continued.
>
> "Is that a problem?", was my reply.
>
> "Not at all", he answered, and went on to introduce himself as Colin.

Colin was what could only be described as 'average'. Average height, average build, average weight, nothing of note in his appearance. Brushed back mousey hair and clean shaven. He looked a few years older than me, probably in his mid-30s. He was English.

> "We had better be off before the car gets towed away", he continued, "I'm parked just round the corner in a 'No Parking' zone."

Colin had brought his car to collect us. It was a 'Paykan', which was actually a Hillman Hunter, a British car, which was assembled in Iran under licence. It was also known as the Iranian Chariot. It was basic, old fashioned, no frills, and was also used as a Taxi, where it was painted yellow!

Colin put our suitcases in the boot of his car and we all piled in.

Colin said he was going to take us to the hotel we would probably be staying in for about a week. He also explained that he was collecting us the following morning, and taking us to see a couple of apartments which were available for us to live in. The hotel was about a half hour drive away.

We set off; the traffic was horrendous! Driving was 'rule of the bumper'. If you were in front, you just put your foot down and hoped the other guy gave way!

After driving for ten minutes, we heard a bang, and felt something hit the back of our car. I was sitting in the front passenger seat and turned to Colin.

"What was that? Has someone hit us?"

"Just a nudge", Colin responded, "We don't even bother stopping for that!"

This was not a good introduction to driving in Tehran!

The hotel was fine. Very average, a bit like Colin.

True to his word, Colin arrived at the hotel at just before 9am the following morning as we were finishing off our breakfast of goat's cheese and freshly baked lavash bread, washed down with a glass of sweet tea without milk. Lavash is a thin bread, similar to an Indian chapati, which is gorgeous when freshly baked. First positive for Iran!

Colin explained that he was the Programming Manager at Melli, and that he worked for me, but was just working out his notice before returning home.

"I've got two apartments for you to see today", volunteered Colin. "There is a big one and a smaller one, and both are on the North side of the city."

"Is that far?". I asked.

"Both are about an hour's drive from here", he responded.

An hour's drive I thought. Will we actually make it that far without incident? Based on the previous evening's experience, I was doubtful.

Colin joined us for a glass of tea before we set off. (In Iran, there is always time for a glass of tea!)

We set off. The hotel was downtown, which was the Southern side of the city. However, we didn't head North, we went East. Colin explained that The Tehran city traffic was so bad that it would take about an hour and a half to drive though the city and cover the ten miles, but if we skirted the city on the motorway, it would take less an hour to get to our destination twenty miles away. We reached the motorway, and the traffic was a lot less, although the driving standard was not good.

We seemed to climb out of the traffic, dust, and humidity the further North we travelled. I had not realised that Tehran was on a hill. The original city started at the southern base of the Alborz mountain range, and gradually was developed to the North, where the summers were cooler and the traffic lighter.

The two apartments were about a mile apart. The first one was quite a small two-bedroom affair on the ground floor, and we were not impressed. It did have access to a small garden, which was shared by five other apartments.

The second apartment was totally different. It was a three story building, and the vacant apartment was the whole middle floor. It was huge! A massive lounge/dining room was 55ft by 29ft (17m by 9m), three large double bedrooms, big kitchen, bathroom, and an additional toilet. There was a central glazed air vent, about ten feet square, which ran the whole height of the building, allowing light to flood in through the multicoloured glass panels. There was also a balcony, and access to the flat roof. The apartment was more than adequately furnished with a five-piece lounge suite, a large oak dining table and twelve chairs, and beds in each room. We were also given a generous amount of money to buy bedding, soft furnishings, and kitchen utensils. We also decided to buy a television.

We said yes to this immediately. We later discovered that the landlord lived on the ground floor, and an American couple, Don and Dee, lived on the upper floor.

That was our accommodation sorted! Just needed our shipment to arrive now.

The Melli Shoe Company paid the rent directly to my landlord. I later discovered that this was almost as much as my salary. I hadn't realised that decent housing was so expensive in Tehran!

We returned to the hotel, where we settled in. The next morning Colin arrived again and said he was taking us shopping for the household items we needed. We spent all day shopping in the more westernised shops, where some staff spoke a little English, but very little. I then realised that the second language in Iran, after its native Farsi, was French.

The following day Colin again appeared.

"Okay. Are you ready?", said he.

"Ready for what?", said I.

"You are moving into your apartment today."

Everything we ordered the day before, including mattresses, were being delivered that day. We also had lots of smaller items in his car.

He took us to our apartment (without having an accident on the way), and left us there. The water and electricity had been switched on, and there were two full gas bottles for the gas cooker.

"You are having the rest of this week to get sorted out", he said, "And you are starting work at the beginning of next week."

It was Wednesday, and the start of next week was Saturday. I worked a five and a half day week, and Thursday afternoon and Friday were the weekend.

Everything we ordered arrived that day. Some by lorry, some by taxi, and some by motor scooter!

We had met the landlord, who spoke only Farsi, and we introduced ourselves to our upstairs neighbours, an American couple, who were both welcoming and very friendly. Over time, we got on very well with them and did some socialising together, although they did prefer their own company in their apartment, drinking vodka.

I was a little concerned at leaving Judi by herself, as she knew no one, but there was a telephone in the apartment, so she could call me for a chat. Antony's school, which was for British children only, and followed a British curriculum, started a week after I started work. Antony was collected on the corner of the street by the school bus, and Judi met a couple of the other British mothers there who lived nearby. Judi also got to meet the wives of the other two English guys I met during the course of my work.

Saturday arrived, and at 7am Colin arrived to pick me up. It was of course the rush hour! I started work at 8:30am, and that was about the time we got there. The Melli offices and computer suite were a little further away than the airport on the opposite side of town to where I lived. Most of the Ex-Pats and wealthy Iranians lived in the cooler North of the city, so this commute was not unusual for many.

Straight in to see Personnel when I got to work. I was given a 'pool' car, as mine was not going to be delivered for another two weeks. I was also told to open a Bank Account in Tehran based bank of my choice, and then shown to my office, which I shared with Fiore, an Iranian lady, who was my Personal Assistant and Secretary. Fiore was Assyrian Iranian, and spoke pretty good English. She was also a Christian. She was tall and thin, at least my height, with almost waist length ginger hair, and blue eyes.

I soon discovered that when you were introduced to someone, the first question asked was:

"What's your Religion?"

I did not know there were so many Religions in the World until I went to Iran. They were all represented there.

Fiore escorted me around the computer suite and the offices annexed to it. To my surprise, I had forty-eight staff. The Computer Operators reported to me, as did the Production Control Staff (the people who set up the job stacks, as I used to do six years previously). Also reporting to me was System Programming, Applications Programming, and the Punch Room (where written data was converted to punch cards). Of these 48 staff, only three spoke English, and twelve spoke French, the remainder spoke Farsi, and a vast array of languages I had never even heard of.

I also found out that the telephone switchboard operators spoke only Farsi. Day one was my first Farsi lesson. There were no direct dial telephones, and to get an outside line to call Judi, I had to tell the switchboard operator my extension number. It was 'see sad o davorzda', 312. Judi also had to ask for this extension when she called me.

When I left IBM, I did say 'I wanted to experience a different culture and way of life', and that is what I was doing!

The work itself did not put me under much pressure, as I knew what I was doing, and had done most of it myself anyway. Communication was a problem! I did not want to stop Fiore doing her work whenever I wanted to speak to somebody who worked for me.

The obvious answer was for me to learn Farsi, but I thought that would take a while, as it was so different to any of the European languages. I decided on a two-pronged approach. Firstly, I would improve my French, which would allow me to speak to about a quarter of my staff, and at the same time learn to speak Farsi. I also discovered that many of my staff wanted to learn English. It's amazing how many of the Iranians I met seem to speak English with a Sunderland accent!

Although four years of French at school gave me only a rudimentary knowledge of the language, within three months I was able to converse, at a fairly basic level with my French speaking staff. However, it took six months to be able to make myself understood in Farsi, but I was almost a fluent Farsi speaker within a year.

Colin left in a few weeks. I never really got to know him. He was unmarried and a bit of a recluse.

Graham was his replacement, and like me, he had been recruited by a Recruitment Agency, and had come over with his wife. He had no children. Graham was about forty years old, and was about an inch taller than me, making him about six feet. He was quite thin with a bit of a stoop. His hair was very thin, and shoulder length, where there was any! He had a huge bald patch. He was a pleasant man. Judi and I got to know him and his wife Sara quite well, and we enjoyed each other's company.

The first month was a bit traumatic for Judi, and she was all for going home! I came in from work one evening, at about my normal time of 7pm.

> "I want to go home!" Judi greeted me with, as I walked through the door.
>
> "What's the problem?", I asked.
>
> "Bloody traffic", says she, "It took me ten minutes to cross the road today when I collected Antony from the school bus. The cars wouldn't stop to let me cross the road!"
>
> It so happened that I knew the solution to this problem, as Fiore had told me how women had to cross the road. It didn't apply to men though!
>
> "You just have to step off the pavement onto the road", I told Judi.
>
> "Are you mad!", she exclaimed. (I was getting used to being called mad by now).
>
> "No", I responded, "The reason this works is because, as a woman, especially with a child, you are classed as a man's property. If you are run over, the driver of the car is liable to pay me a lot of money. The amount would be determined by a Court, but it would be more than only a wealthy driver could afford."

Judi, very cautiously, tried this the next day. The traffic screeched to a halt, and she was able to just stroll across the road. This did help her somewhat, but she was still not enjoying her new environment. I agreed we would review things in three months, and if she still wanted to go home, we would.

After another two months, Judi had made so many new friends, and we were socialising so much, she was loving it.

Antony made new friends at school, and seemed to spend most of the summer evenings in the street on his skateboard with his friends. Most weekends we were out visiting friends as a family, or having friends around our apartment. I would occasionally join a few of the guys down the local pub, 'The Half Crown', for a game of darts and a beer.

After I had worked for Melli for a month, it was payday!

When I worked for IBM, I was given a monthly payslip on the 20th of the month, and my salary was credited to my bank account on the same day.

It was a bit different in the World of Melli. I was given a piece of paper which had my monthly salary written on it, but it was not an actual payslip, nor was my salary paid into my bank account. The procedure was to take your piece of paper to a nearby bank, where you were paid cash! It was a particular bank, as it was owned by Melli.

Everybody was 'paid' at the same time, and the bank closed at 3pm, so almost everyone was at the bank at lunch time.

I waited in line with a couple of the Iranian guys who worked for me to get my cash. It was my turn at the bank teller's counter. He said something I didn't understand.

> "Pardon", I said, followed by "I don't understand", in my clearest English.
>
> "Englander?", he replied.
>
> "Yes, I don't speak Farsi. Do you speak English?" was my response.
>
> "Little", the teller retorted. "Identification."
>
> "What identification?", I said.
>
> "Passport", he returned.

I didn't have my passport, as Melli kept the passports of all their foreign workers, and I didn't have a Driver's Licence yet. I was booked in to get that the following week.

"I don't have it. It's with Melli", I answered.

"You have any other identification?" responded the bank clerk.

I didn't have anything, not even a letter saying who I worked for, or where I was living. I had no correspondence of any kind with me.

Then I suddenly thought, I have a passport size photo of myself, which was for my Drivers Licence application. With as much self-assurance as I could muster, I took it out of my wallet and thrust it at him.

"Here's my identification", I confidently announced.

He looked at it, looked at me, looked at the photo again, looked at me again, turned the photo over and looked at the back, which was blank, and said,

"That's okay", and handed over a huge wad of cash to me!

Everybody who I was with was amazed. I'd found a chink in the banks security system. All you need to do is carry a photograph of yourself around with you!

It was shortly after my first payday that our possessions arrived from the UK. The three weeks had actually taken six weeks, the last three were waiting for Customs clearance. However, everything arrived, and there were absolutely no breakages. This was definitely due to Judi's meticulous packing, as the boxes were just thrown out of the large open truck which delivered them to a guy standing on the pavement, who dropped about half of them, some actually bounced down the steps to our apartment. It was a very haphazard affair, culminating with the two delivery men standing with their hands out awaiting their tip.

Judi was a lot happier now, as was Antony, as his toys were also in the shipment!

My new car arrived three days after I started my new job.

I had been driving the 'pool car' before this, but I wasn't too impressed with it. It didn't have much in the way of interior refinement, just knobs that looked like they were from a previous age, and fitted in random places. The engine lacked power, the gearbox was very clunky, and the suspension was totally inadequate for the potholes in the roads, and it was covered in dents.

My new car was exactly the same, without the dents!

In my first month I had only one minor accident. I was told that all accidents had to be reported to the Melli Transport Department, who just shrugged it off. I went to the Transport Manager and said to him,

> "I've had a bash in my rear door."
>
> "We'll make a note of it", said the man from the Melli Transport Department.
>
> "What do I do about getting it repaired?", I ventured.
>
> "Nothing, at the moment", Transport responded, "We normally wait until there are five or six before we bother getting them repaired."

That actually didn't take that long! During my year and a half in Iran I had seventeen accidents, one being a serious one.

My working hours at Melli were 8:30am until 5:15pm, with a forty-five-minute lunch break. Lunch was provided free of charge to all employees in the staff restaurant from Saturday to Wednesday. Thursday was a half day, when we finished at 1:15pm, so no lunch was provided. In fact, the restaurant was not open on weekends, although sometimes the computer was processing jobs which were late.

Lunch was a little monotonous, being the same on Saturday through to Tuesday. Starter was plain yoghurt with garlic; the main course was Sabzi (Herb Stew) and a whole boiled aubergine; dessert was plain yoghurt, with sugar, if you wanted it.

As a special treat, on Wednesdays, especially for the foreign workers, we had fish & chips!

We had been in Iran for about two months, and I needed a haircut! Although Judi was okay for westerner style Ladies Hairdressers, I had never seen a Gents Hairdresser. I asked some of the guys at work about this. The only two Brits I knew were Graham, who didn't bother having his hair cut, and Harvey, an Accountant, who was totally bald. I decided to ask one of my Computer Operators who spoke English. He was called Aslan, and was a Turkish Sunni Muslim. He was dark skinned, dark haired, dark eyed, slightly built, and had a thick black moustache. His haircut looked okay.

"I'll take you to my barber after work, if you want", he offered.

"Is it far?" I asked.

"Five-minute drive from work", was his response.

"Will he be open after we finish work?" I enquired.

"Yes, he doesn't close until it gets dark", was Aslan's reply.

'Gets dark !!', I thought. Must be because electricity is so expensive here. (Which it was.)

We left the office in Aslan's car, immediately turned off the main road, and zig-zagged through the busy narrow dirt roads for about ten minutes.

"We're here!", Aslan announced, pulling to one side of the road. Cars and motorcycles were zipping around all over the dusty, dirt road, which didn't seem to have a footpath of any sort.

Amongst the traffic was a barber's chair! Right in the middle of the road. Aslan's barber friend was at work among the dust and traffic, clipping away at a customer's hair.

I was next, and with some apprehension, took my seat in the middle of the road, with cars and motorcycles narrowly missing me, to have my haircut, and my beard and ears trimmed as well! It was a good haircut, done with mechanical clippers, and a cigarette lighter, which he used for burning the hairs off my ears, without actually burning me. I continued going there for the rest of my time in Tehran. I also understood why he closed when it got dark!

After we had been living in Tehran for about four months, the British School asked Judi if she would like a part-time job as an Administrative Assistant. She jumped at the chance, as she would meet even more people, and wouldn't be at home most of the time by herself. It was getting too cold now for sunbathing on the balcony, which was her favourite pastime.

Judi was tasked with doing a bit of typing and helping out in office, which she really enjoyed. We also met many British couples through her job, and we socialised a lot.

Judi had now conquered the Tehran Taxi system. Taxis in Tehran operated in a way I have never encountered before. It was possible to phone for a taxi to pick you up from home, but street numbers and sometimes names were not displayed, and this service was unreliable and quite expensive.

However, there were literally hundreds of taxis in the city, and each one had their set route which was North to South, or West to East, along every major road in the city. You just walked to the nearest main road, which was two minutes from our apartment, and waved down one of the bright orange taxis, which were mostly Paykan's. Our main road was a North-South one. If there was room in the taxi (one in the front and three in the back), you got in. You paid the driver the standard charge, which was ten rials (about 8p), and got off at an intersecting junction for the West-East part of your journey, and repeated the process with another taxi.

Judi and I both thought it was a great system, and you could get almost anywhere in the city for 16p!

This was, of course, over forty years ago, so I would expect things have changed a lot since then.

While sitting at my desk at work in November 1977, I received a hand delivered letter. I'd never had a letter hand delivered before so I was naturally surprised. I opened it to find it was an Invitation. It was a request to attend a Buffet Lunch at Mr. Irvani's cottage. Mr. Irvani was my boss! He was Chairman (and Owner) of the Melli Industrial Group, which was everything to do with shoes in Iran. He owned over 300 shoe shops in Iran, the factories where the shoes were made, the tanneries where the leather was processed, and the farms where the cattle came from. All of his businesses were computerised, and all the data processing was done on the IBM 370 computer I was responsible for running.

Mr. Irvani was believed to be the second richest man in Iran, second only to Mohammed Reza Pahlavi, the Shah of Persia!

And he invited Judi, Antony, and I to a social event. Even better, it was on a Thursday, so I was given the day off work to attend.

The day of Mr. Irvani's Buffet Lunch came round. We were given a map to help us find the cottage, which was in the north-western outskirts of the city, about a half hour drive away.

The 'cottage' was not as I expected! Judi had the map and was instructing me which way to go.

"We are here!", Judi exclaimed quite abruptly.

"There's nothing here", I said looking around.

"You've gone past it", she responded.

"There's nothing here", I repeated, "Just a brick wall".

"You drove past the gate", Judi explained, "It's that huge iron one we've just past. Doesn't look like it goes anywhere, but the plate on the gate says 'Irvani Cottage'."

At that point I noticed a couple of other cars behind us, who seemed to be lost. One of them was Graham. I got out of the car and walked over to him.

"Is this it, do you think?", I said.

"Guess so", replied Graham, "We had better look inside."

We went to the gate, which automatically opened to admit us. I noticed the surveillance cameras just inside the gate, and there was a road heading up a slight incline.

At the top of the incline, we could see the 'cottage'. It was actually a mansion, which probably had about ten bedrooms. It was massive. Beyond the cottage were the grounds, which were several acres and accessed by a footbridge over a river.

The story was that Mr. Irvani wanted a stream at the bottom of his garden, but there wasn't one, so he had a river diverted and a bridge built across it. I'm not sure if the story is true or not, but it's something I could easily believe.

As we got closer, we saw the car park, with staff showing us to our parking places. We also saw Mr. Irvani's' three Rolls Royce cars which he was using as courtesy cars for his more distinguished guests.

In the grounds there were five quite large buildings, which were for his guests to eat, apart from the huge restaurant area in the house itself. The house restaurant served a vast array of Persian meals and desserts, being served at 2pm. The other five buildings each had its own kitchen with staff, and had covered and open dining areas. Each of the kitchens cooked a different dish, and all had ample salad and fruit available. These kitchens served individually dedicated foods, which were American, English, German, Chicken Kebab and a separate kitchen which served beverages and desserts. These kitchens were open from 11am until 5pm, just in case you didn't want to eat in the house restaurant, or wanted a snack during the day!

It was a tradition that each November, Mr. Irvani had one of these Buffet Lunches for all of his Senior Managers and his senior foreign workers.

It started to snow in mid-December. When it snowed, it snowed heavily, ten centimetres overnight was not uncommon. The main problem was that the roads were not cleared! Announcements were made on the television and in the newspapers when the snow started to fall to tell drivers to fit their studded winter tyres. If you were caught by the police without them, you were fined, and your car was confiscated until you fitted them. As the snow got deeper and deeper, and more compacted over the weeks it was advisable to fit snow chains to your car, which most Expats did, and most locals did not. Accidents quadrupled during the two months of snow.

However, the snow was good fun on the weekends, when groups of us went to the ski slopes just a few miles north of the city. Three or four families went together, but not many of us could actually ski, including me. I overcame this problem by taking a large truck inner tube which we could sit in and slide down the more gentle slopes.

"I want to go first", Antony said as we pulled up at the parking area.

"No!", I replied, "I'd better just try it out first.", which I did.

I took the inner tube about half way up one of the gentle slopes and gave it a 'test run' before letting Antony have a go. Antony was just approaching his eleventh birthday, and Judi was insistent that he should make it without injury!

All of the guys, and a couple of the children and ladies had a go. Naturally, Antony thought it was great, and he had a couple of goes, then I had a couple of goes, then we had a couple of goes together. It was great fun!

The guys were, of course, competitive, and we each tried to go as far as we could, stopping as close to the chain link fence at the bottom of the slope as we could. Well, I thought, it's my tube, so I'm going to go the furthest! I took the tube up to the top of the slope, pushed off, and jumped in. It gathered speed very quickly and I had no control whatsoever over my descent rate. I hurtled down the hill, speeding towards the fence, with a look of bravado, whilst inwardly hoping I would get a puncture and stop dead. I didn't get a puncture. I didn't stop. Not even when I reached the chain link fence. I had reached the fence where there was a hole at the bottom. Still speeding out of control, I ducked to avoid my head hitting the fence.

The other side of the fence was the highway, which luckily was not very busy, as I hurtled across it and came to an abrupt halt at the chain link fence at the other side of the road. I hit the fence at an angle with my left shoulder taking most of the impact. My shoulder hurt, and didn't look quite right.

A couple of the guys came to my rescue. One was a nurse, who I didn't know very well, took one look at my shoulder, and announced,

> "It's dislocated!"
>
> "I know it bloody hurts!", was my whimpering response. "Do I have to go to the hospital?"
>
> "Not necessary", replied the Nurse from Hell, as he took my arm and twisted it into a position it had never been in before, "I've fixed it!"

I thought it hurt before he touched it, but now I was in excruciating pain. I was helped across the road after giving the tube a good kick, where I was given a couple of aspirin by the 'nurse', and told to just sit quietly in my car. Amazingly, after about thirty minutes the pain became bearable, and as was our usual routine, we went to the 'Mexical' restaurant on the way home for a pizza and a couple of pints.

My shoulder felt okay after a few days, although all around it was painful for several weeks, but it was forty years later that I discovered why it hurt for so long!

We were later surprised to find out that Mr. Irvani also had a Christmas lunch for his senior Christian staff. Judi and I were also invited to this, and Christmas Day was given as a holiday to most of Melli's Christian staff. This was a very lavish affair which was held in the restaurant in Mr Irvani's cottage. No turkey or pork was served, but practically everything else was! We also received a Christmas present from Mr. Irvani of a small Iranian rug.

As we moved into 1978, we were feeling really at home in Tehran. We had made lots of friends, both Iranian and European, since our arrival in the previous July. I quite enjoyed my work, and was becoming familiar to things unaccustomed to us. The drive to work was a bit of a nightmare because of the poor driving and perpetual traffic jams. I decided that, to save time in the mornings, I would not have breakfast before leaving home. As it normally took about seventy-five minutes to drive the eighteen miles to work, and there was a two-mile unavoidable stretch which was always almost stationery, I would have breakfast on the way.

However, this did not mean pulling over into a service area (they didn't exist), but buying breakfast from street vendors who had set up their businesses by the side of the congested part of the road. The vendors normally had fruit or cheese in the Summer, and roasted nuts or hot beetroot in the Winter.

As you were crawling along the road, a vendor would come up to the car window.

> "Breakfast?", he would say. Most vendors recognised 'foreigners', and had enough basic English or French to do business!
>
> "What have you today?", I'd enquire.
>
> "Beetroot", he responded, which was my favourite winter breakfast.
>
> "Yek bazorg" (large one), I would say, just showing off my Farsi, so he didn't rip me off.

He would scurry off to his little catering van, and two minutes later he would appear with a plate of steaming beetroot cut into cubes, and a fork. I paid him, which was normally twenty rials (16p), and he scurried off looking for another customer. I was still slowly driving along the road. When I had finished eating my beetroot, I stuck my arm out of the window, and he ran over to retrieve his plate and fork, and hopefully went to wash it before serving his next customer. In this time, I had probably travelled a few hundred yards. If the traffic was a bit lighter than normal and I had travelled further, he would get his plate and fork back the next morning!

A nice hot breakfast in the cold mornings, and a bit of a break from a tedious journey.

Apart from my annual holidays at Melli, I also had the local holidays. These were mostly religious (Muslim), and mostly 'sad', but there was at least one a month. The problem with 'sad' holidays was that everywhere closed, and even the television played depressing sombre music all day and night.

Sad holidays often involved processions through the main streets of the city with hundreds of people flagellating themselves. Definitely not my idea of a holiday. We would normally take a picnic up to the mountains for the day, often with a few friends, or join Don and Dee upstairs from us for a few beers or vodkas! Don and I would play chess, badly, after a few drinks, and the ladies would chat. Antony would often go round to a friend's house, or his friend would come to us.

We had a television, which was quite unusual for foreigners. There was only one channel, which seemed to broadcast Iranian soaps for most of the time. There was about an hour a day which was in English, but the programs were very restricted, and censored. An early evening News in English was broadcast for about fifteen minutes, but there was no International news, just local news, which was mainly what the Shah had done that day. Two other programs were mainly broadcast for the rest of the hour, Little House on the Prairie, and a Flintstones cartoon. The television never really got used a lot!

The most interesting part of watching television was just before the 7pm News started. There was a clock on the screen, as used to be the case on the television in England, which showed the time a minute or so before the News started. The interesting bit was that the clock was never quite right, until a large finger appeared and pushed the pointer round, so the News always started dead on time.

As the winter gave way to summer, we attended many social events with friends, and some had swimming pools, so pool parties were very popular. Alcohol was legal in 1978, and there was even a local brewery called 'Shams', which brewed a perfectly acceptable lager. There was also imported beer available, and Don, my neighbour, seemed to have unlimited access to vodka at 70p a bottle!

Although I always had a supply of beer at home, I never drank it directly from the bottle, although most of my friends did. There was a reason for this. After living in Tehran for only a few months, I was at a friend's house, and we were having a few bottles of beer.

> "Another one?", asked Bruce, as he was polishing off his second bottle.
>
> "Of course,", I replied, as I swigged the remainder of my second bottle.
>
> "I'll just get a couple of cold ones out of the fridge", Bruce mumbled as he went to the kitchen.

He appeared a few minutes later with a bottle in each hand. He flipped the crown cap off each of the brown beer bottles and handed me one as he took a swig from the other.

> "Cheers!", says he.
>
> "Bottoms Up!", I responded, following his lead.

Suddenly, I thought I was going to choke! Something was in my throat which wasn't beer. I gagged and coughed, and a lump was in my mouth. I spat it out. It was a mouse's head!

Since that day I have never drank out of anything I could not see into!

As I have already mentioned, the traffic in Tehran was atrocious. Even the extremes used by the traffic police seemed to have little effect on the drivers. Ignoring traffic lights, or jumping the lights was very common, even when there was a traffic policeman there controlling the crossroads. A couple of times I saw the policeman lose his temper, and any car which had stuck its nose over the white line had its headlights smashed by the policeman's truncheon! This didn't seem to be a deterrent.

Traffic had become a major problem in Tehran. The air in the downtown part of the city was thick and acrid, with some of the highest pollution rates in the World. The Government came up with a solution. They decided to half the amount of traffic entering the city centre by restricting vehicles by their registration number. Odd numbers one day, followed by even numbers the next, as a permanent fix. On the face of it, it seems a draconian, but effective solution. However, the wealthier Iranians just bought another car with either an odd or even number plate, depending on the plate on their current car.

The less scrupulous just had a different set of number plates made, which they changed on their car as required.

I know this system was introduced, but I don't know for how long, or how effective it was.

My car accidents were progressing at a steady one a month, but in July 1978 I was involved in a more serious one. I was waiting at a wide junction for the traffic to ease so I could join a main highway. I was well behind the white 'stop' line, patiently waiting for an opportunity to merge in with the traffic.

A large American style petrol tanker came hurtling past me at about 60mph, but swerved as he was level with me, which caused his trailer to hook the front of my car, spinning my car around and backwards into the trailer's rear wheels. It occurred so quickly I didn't realise what was happening. The rear of my car was crushed by the first set of wheels on the trailer's rear double axle. The car twisted and went under the wheels of the second axle, which crushed the front of the car and finally pushed it to the side of the road, where it stopped, resting on the passenger side.

Cars stopped and people came running over to get me out. The petrol tank had split, with fuel running all over the road, and pieces of the hot engine were lying amongst the other debris of twisted metal and broken glass. My helpers had trouble opening the driver's door as it was caved in and jammed solid. There was no glass left in any of the windows, and I was pulled out through where the front windscreen used to be, and carried about fifty yards down the road, where they lay me on the dirt verge of the road.

I was semi-conscious and lay there for what seemed an eternity until an ambulance arrived, by which time I had recovered somewhat, but I was shaking with shock. I was taken to the nearest hospital for examination, but felt fine by the time we arrived there. My only injuries were a deep cut on one of my fingers, and superficial scratches and scrapes to my face. I was told that if I had been carrying a passenger, they most certainly would have died!

Although the car was what we would have called a 'write-off', it was actually repaired. Not much of the original was in the repaired car, and when it rained the wheel wells and boot filled with water, and it seemed to drift a little to one side when driven.

I consider that to be the seventh of my lives to have been used.

That summer was when the 'discontent' seemed to start among the working class Iranians. Iran was very much a 'have' and a 'have not' society. Although Melli encouraged its staff not to discuss salaries, it did of course happen. Probably because it was discouraged!

I was truly amazed at the differences in people's pay. The Expats all seemed to earn a similar salary, within about 10%. However, the fifty or so people who worked for me earned only about one-tenth of my salary. My immediate manager, Farshadfah, who was an Iranian from one of the wealthier families, and actually knew very little about anything to do with computers, earned about ten times my salary! This was about one hundred times the salary of my computer operators or programming staff. I sensed that this disparity would sooner, rather than later, lead to problems within the country.

The News on radio and television was heavily censored, so nothing of the unrest which had started taking place in the country was ever broadcast. It was well before the days of mobile phones or the Internet, and also many in the Expat community did not mix in Iranian society.

Rumours of riots in the city of Qom in January 1978 started to reach us in the Spring of that year. Also, disturbances in Tabriz in February. The Qom demonstrations were by religious students from the University, who objected to a local newspaper accusing the Mullah, Ayatollah Khomeini of being a British Agent who was trying to make Iran a Communist country, which everyone I spoke to thought was ridiculous.

People started to die in these demonstrations, and the USA was held partially to blame because President Carter would not approve the export of tear gas and rubber bullets to Iran, so the Shahs troops used live rounds when controlling the demonstrations or riots. There were a few small demonstrations in Tehran in March, April, and June, but it was generally thought this was to do with pay. It proved to be a lot more than that, as we soon discovered.

I am going to write a little about what happened at the time of the build up before the Iranian Revolution, through my own experiences and those of people I knew. This is not a history of the start of the Iranian Revolution, just my own personal views. If the reader wants to know more about the Iranian Revolution, there are numerous books on the subject. This is only a record of my experiences.

The incident that first seemed to start the demonstrations in

Tehran was the Rex cinema fire in Abadan, (a town 600 miles to the South of Tehran), in August. There were about five hundred people in the cinema, someone barred the doors from the outside, and set the cinema alight. Over four hundred died. The Government blamed the Revolutionary terrorists, and vice versa. I believe the blame is still not resolved, although one person, with allegiance to neither, has admitted to starting the fire.

At this time, I was beginning to think this is probably going to deteriorate, and is not the best place to be for me and my family. I went to see my boss at Melli,

> "I think this country is becoming politically unstable, and I would like to leave", I told Farshadfah.
>
> "Rubbish!", he responded, "It will just blow over, it always does."
>
> "I'm not happy about my family being here, and I would like to leave", I repeated.
>
> "You are on a three-year contract", was Farshadfah's reply.
>
> "But this looks like the build up to a Revolution, to me", I retorted, "Surely the contract is void?".
>
> "You can only leave by breaking your contract, which means you have to give three months' notice, and make your own arrangements to get home, at your own expense." was Farshadfah's ultimatum.

I went directly to Personnel, who confirmed this.

My three months' notice was handed in that day.

The following day Judi and I went to the Travel Agent in town and I purchased our airline tickets home for mid-November. British Airways, direct flight, bought and paid for on the spot.

At least I'd got three months to look for another job, so I started looking immediately. I saw an advertisement in the only English language paper in Tehran for a job with an American company in Saudi Arabia as an Operations Manager at the Jeddah University. I applied for it, and in late August I went for an interview in the

Sheraton hotel.

"Where can I find Mr. Zelkas", I asked a smartly dressed youth at the hotel reception. He understood me perfectly, and replied,

"Are you Mr. Covelle? He's waiting for you in the lounge. I'll arrange for some tea to be sent over."

Mr. Zelkas greeted me cordially with a smile and a broad Texas accent. He was about six feet tall, heavy set, but not fat, light close cropped Military style hair, clean shaven, and wearing a smart suit. He informed me he worked for a company called Electronic Data Systems (EDS), which I had never heard of.

"What attracted you to this job?", was his first question.

"I've always wanted to work in Saudi Arabia", I lied. He accepted my answer at face value without question. After quite a lengthy interview, and two lots of tea and biscuits, Mr. Zelkas said,

"When could you start, if the position was offered to you?"

"Mid November", I responded, and explained that I had to work my three months' notice.

"That would be perfect", said Mr. Zelkas, "The contract with the University starts on 1st December", he then paused before saying,

"Do you want the job?".

I gave a positive response, and he said he would keep in contact, and a contract would be drawn up within a few days. I now had a job to go to when I left Iran, and, again, it was a 'different' sort of place.

I recall 4th September 1978, as it was the last day of Ramadan, and I was asked to lots of parties by my Iranian friends to celebrate

the end of fasting by eating vast quantities of food, and in some cases, drinking too much beer. Something I've never had a problem with.

It was also less than two weeks to my birthday and Judi and I were deciding which of the more expensive restaurants to celebrate in, or if we should have a party at home.

There was a big prayer meeting arranged for that day, somewhere downtown, and about 400,000 people were expected to attend. Most of my Muslim staff were going to attend. It seems that the Mullah (Preacher type guy) who was running the show decided to make the event a march through the city instead, which got out of hand, and there were a few skirmishes with the police.

On the following Friday, 8th September, there was a rally of workers in Jaleh Square, which was close to where a friend of mine lived, who I was visiting. His apartment was in one of the streets leading to Jaleh Square. There were three of us just chatting and drinking beer, and we could hear the rally going on outside. It sounded like things were getting a little rowdy and out of control. It was then that we heard multiple loud bangs, which seemed to go on for ages. We all had the same thought.

"Is that gunfire?", asked Mohammed rhetorically.

"I hope not!", responded George.

"Not a chance.", I conjectured, "Probably just fireworks."

After a while we decided to venture out, just to see what had been happening.

The three of us furtively walked down the street from Mohammed's home, towards the square. The street was deserted, but as we approached the square, we could hear wailing and sobbing together with angry raised voices. It was only about twenty yards from the square when I looked down and could see blood running down the street gutter. We all froze, went very quiet, our faces became drawn, and we all became very frightened and uncomfortable being in the street. Turning around and quietly, we returned to the apartment without travelling any further. We never actually got as far as Jaleh Square, but later heard what had happened.

There were about 5,000 people in the square who were demonstrating against the Shah, I was told the next day. The crowd got out of control, and the Government troops did not have any riot control equipment or knowledge of how to control a riot situation. They did what they thought was the only thing they could do. They fired live bullets, firstly above the heads of the demonstrators, then into the crowd. About one hundred people died, and the massacre was later referred to as 'Black Friday'.

This was also the day Martial Law was declared.

The following day was the start of the strikes throughout Iran. Tehran was particularly badly affected, as all the Government offices closed. The Melli offices remained open, and we continued working as normal, despite a large number of Melli's shoe shops being closed, and some shoe factories being on strike. A curfew was imposed throughout Tehran, and nobody was allowed outside between 6pm and 6am, unless they had a permit. No one I knew had a permit!

I didn't go to a restaurant for my birthday, but instead we had a 'stopover' party, which went on until 6am, where about thirty people stayed for the whole night!

Things started to get pretty bad for foreigners, especially the Americans, or anyone who looked American!

Slogans were painted on doors and walls where Americans were thought to live, including where I lived.

'Go Home Yanky', seemed to be the favourite. Several cars were burned, and abuse was hurled at foreigners by people who were previously friendly Iranians. Our local corner shop would serve me and Judi, but not Don and Dee, our American neighbours.

Both Don and myself still drove to our respective places of employment. He worked for an American helicopter company at the opposite side of the city to me, and told me how a lorry forced him off the road on his way to work one morning, whilst the occupants hurled abuse at him.

My own experiences were a bit more scary!

One morning on my drive to work, before reaching the main highway, I became aware of small plumes of dust appearing in front of me in the road. Although a little confused as to what it was, I didn't pay it much heed. It happened three days in a row, and always in the same spot. On the fourth day, at the same spot, I heard a loud crack which seemed to emanate from within the car. I pulled over to investigate, thinking that maybe something in the boot was rattling around, but could see nothing amiss. I just continued on my way to work listening for any noises or bangs which could signify a problem with my (now very battered) Paykan.

I thought nothing of the incident until about a week later when I was having my car washed. This was a weekly occurrence carried out for a few rials by one of the office cleaning staff.

> "Mr. Jeff, Mr. Jeff!" Abdul shouted at me in an agitated manner, "Come see!".

That was about the extent of his English, but he came over to me and grabbed me by the arm and led me to where he was washing my car.

> "Look see!", he continued pointing at a hole in the bodywork of my car, just behind the rear door, near the petrol filler cap. Naively, I thought vandals had been out to damage my car even more than it already was. I just waved it aside, but Abdul became even more agitated, and ran off! He went to my boss, Farshadfah, who he dragged out to where I was still standing by my car. The two of them were speaking in Farsi, which was far too fast for me to understand.
>
> Farshadfah came over to the car and examined the hole. He then turned to me and said,
>
> "That's a bullet hole!"

"What!", I gasped, "Who has done that?".

It then clicked in my brain. The noise I heard a few days earlier was the car being hit by a bullet, and the previous 'plumes of dust' in the road were either just practice shots, or the marksman wasn't very good.

"Another couple of centimetres", said Farshadfar, "And that bullet would have hit your petrol tank, or another meter and it would have hit you!".

I was disturbed, to say the least. I had been told of snipers in the city, but they were purported to be in the South of the city, not the North. I changed my route to work the next day.

It seems that when my company car was returned a few weeks later, it was the only one ever returned with a bullet hole in it!

In early November there was a major conflict between university students and troops in Tehran, which resulted in an even more stringent curfew, closing practically everything during the day, as well as strict enforcement of the 6pm deadline. Amazingly, through all of the demonstrations and conflict that was going on, there were never any power cuts. The logic being that this would have a greater detrimental effect to the working class than the 'upper' class, so the power workers did not join in the strike, but did support it.

The other scary experience I had was when visiting my local petrol station. It happened only a week before we left Tehran.

The earlier strikes had now escalated to a point, in early November, where a General Strike was declared. This affected fuel supplies, since the oil fields and refineries were on strike. Consequently, there was a shortage of fuel in the petrol stations. This led to rationing, which, I think, was 20 litres a visit.

There were really not that many petrol stations in Tehran, considering the amount of traffic there was. Queues to buy fuel were very long, and the waiting time in the queue was two to three hours. I needed to fill-up twice a week, so it was definitely an inconvenience, which added another two or three hours to an already long day.

The petrol station I went to was guarded by three soldiers, who attempted to keep order among some of the very irate drivers waiting in the mile long queue down the main road. The soldiers were getting angry and frustrated, as drivers were shouting at the customers already at the pumps to hurry up, and things got worse as the pumps started to run out one by one.

I was about tenth in line, and wondering whether I was actually going to get any petrol before it ran out, when a car came hurtling down from the back of the queue and pushed in behind one of the cars which was refuelling. He jumped out shouting that he was in a hurry, and had to get some fuel now. Several of the drivers in the cars nearby jumped out, and a scuffle ensued.

The soldiers waded in with their rifle butts to break up the fight, dragged the offending queue jumper from the pack, stood him up against the wall of the garage, and shot him dead!

His body was left on the ground and all the drivers returned quietly to their cars and waited patiently for their turn at the petrol pumps.

After about twenty minutes, it was my turn. I purchased my twenty litres of petrol and drove home.

Judi said I was very quiet for the rest of that evening when I returned home.

It was mid-November, and getting pretty close to the end of my notice period with Melli. As my flight was now only about a week away, I thought I had better check with Personnel how things were going and process my leaving documentation.

> “Hi, Rashid”, I greeted the Personnel employee cheerily, “How’s my exit paperwork doing?”.

I knew bureaucracy was always a bit of a problem, but since I had to buy my own tickets home, and arrange my own shipment of my personal effects, there wouldn't be any issues.

I was wrong!

> "There is a problem, Jeff", replied Rashid. "All the Government offices are on strike, and we cannot get an Exit Visa until they reopen".
>
> "So, what do we have to do?", I responded with some apprehension.
>
> "Nothing we can do until they reopen", said Rashid, "whenever that will be!".
>
> "But my flight home is booked for next week!", I spluttered, to which Rashid responded, "That probably won't happen. You cannot leave without an Exit Visa, and the airport workers are also on strike!"
>
> "So, I'm stuck here until things are resolved, and it looks like things are going to get a lot worse before they get better", I said despairingly, and asked if there is anything at all I could do to get around the problem. Rashid told me there was nothing, and gave me our Passports back.
>
> "There is no point Melli having your Passports", Rashid said, "I won't be able to process it before your leaving date, and then you will have to sort it out yourself!"

I was at a loss what to do. I had arranged for our personal possessions to be collected by the Shippers the day before we were due to leave in about a week's time.

I took our Passports and decided that I would try to sort things out the following day. Not many staff were turning up for work, so it was a struggle to continue operating the computer, and I couldn't really do anything. As I now had all three passports, I decided my time would be better spent trying to sort out my exit from Iran.

I never returned to work.

Later that day I contacted Mr. Zelkas to see if he could help us. Unfortunately, not, but he did give me the EDS address in Jeddah, Saudi Arabia, where my shipment should be sent.

The following day was spent at the Government offices downtown. I achieved absolutely nothing! The few people who I found on the premises just told me there was nothing to be done until the strike was over. I thought we could be stuck here for another two or three weeks yet, miss our flight, and maybe not get to Saudi Arabia until mid-December!

As it turned out, the strike continued until the middle of January, but I didn't know that.

I also went to the airport to see what the situation was there. It was pretty grim. The only people working were the foreign airlines staff, and Customs was manned by the Military. There were no baggage handling staff working, and the airport arrival and departure timetable was none existent. A small number of flights were arriving and departing erratically.

After a couple of days trying to find out what was happening, I found out nothing. I checked with some of my none Iranian friends to see what they were doing. Most had decided to just sit tight for the moment. A few had decided to drive to the Iraqi border at Abadan, and try to drive the thirty miles across Southern Iraq to the Kuwaiti border, where they knew it would be safe, perhaps!

I tried to contact the British Embassy, but without much luck. I Knew one of the Embassy staff who said that the advice was to just stay at home until things quietened down, and there is no way the Embassy could help with an Exit Visa.

I was in a dilemma. No Exit Visa and it's probable that our flight might not even materialise. What the Hell was I going to do?

Antony's school had closed, and I was also at home, and Judi was worried. We spent the next couple of days packing our possessions for the Shipping Company, who quite surprisingly, turned up at the agreed day and time to collect them, and threw them rather haphazardly into the back of an open truck. The guy in charge told us it would normally take about two weeks to get it to Saudi Arabia, but could be longer because of the strikes.

The following evening was our flight. Although I had our passports, mine should have had an Exit Visa stamped in it, which also covered Judi and Antony. The Exit Visa should have been stamped on the next page in my passport to where the Entry Visa was. I knew I could not get past Airport Customs and Immigrations without the Exit Visa, so I glued the pages of my passport together where the Exit Visa would have been! I had nothing to lose if this was discovered, so worth a gamble.

We only had hand luggage and I decided we would get to the airport early and park in the airport car park. We were there at 7am, which was twelve hours before our flight. I parked in the car park, and left a note on the windscreen saying the car was the property of the Melli Shoe Company. I was unable to contact Melli, as no one was answering the phone. I assumed the switchboard staff were also on strike.

We headed to the airport check-in area. It was absolutely packed, people seemed to be rushing around all over the place in total confusion. Almost everyone looked worried and distressed. We pushed our way over to the British Airways check-in desk, just to find it unmanned. I wasn't too perturbed, as we were twelve hours early and I didn't really expect the check-in desk to be open yet. I looked around to find a flight information board which was working, as most were not. Checking through the flights listed, I noticed that most of them appeared to have been cancelled, including our flight to Heathrow!!

This seemed an appropriate time to panic, but luckily, I didn't.

The whole check-in area was absolute mayhem. Civilian staff seemed to be attempting control check-in, but not doing a very good job. The luggage handling staff were on strike, so everyone was carrying their suitcases. People were pushing past the desks onto the luggage handling conveyors, which were not working, and trying to get to the airside part of the airport using the stationery conveyor belts as pathways. Staff were attempting to stop them, and fights were breaking out, which the civilian police were endeavouring to control. People had tickets in their hands and were thrusting them in the face of any official who was nearby. I noticed that some people were allowed through the check-in area by officials, if they paid a bribe, and the official didn't even look at the ticket. This was obviously the way to get to the next level, which was Security, which was being controlled by the Military.

I had recently been paid, and had a pocket full of US Dollars. I had converted most of my rials into US Dollars over the last three months.

Selecting what looked to be the official who seemed to care the least, I pushed through the crowd to him, with Judi and Antony in tow. I showed him our tickets, which had a $50 bill sticking out of the top, he removed the bill, and allowed us through to the Security area without even glancing at the tickets.

We were now, unofficially checked though to a non-existent flight, but one step at a time.

The next step was to get through Security to the boarding gates. Soldiers were controlling the security gates, but they were not really sure what they were supposed to do, other than check Iranians had passports, and foreigners had passports with Exit Visas in them. There were only three soldiers and dozens of people pressing forward and shouting at them. One of the soldiers looked particularly flustered, almost to the point of panic, so I selected him to approach. Barging my way through the crowd I thrust my passport under his nose,

> "My flight's leaving now!", I shouted at him, appearing panicked. He fumbled with my passport as at least three other people were pushing their passports at him urgently.
>
> "Hurry up!", I screamed at him, "I'm going to miss the flight".
>
> "Slowly, slowly", he said, fumbling with the passport, unable to open it at the correct page.
>
> "Quickly, quickly", I responded, "My flight has been called!". The next people in line were also shouting at him to hurry up.

He could not get the pages apart, and in frustration, he threw my passport back to me and waved us through. My heart rate had at least doubled, and I was sweating profusely, but we were through to the departure area. Pity we didn't have a flight!

At this point I had no idea what to do. All dressed up and nowhere to go, one would say.

I had three British Airways flight tickets in my hand for a cancelled flight. There was only one flight in, which I think was going to Kuwait, and there were dozens of people just milling around. People just seemed to be crowding around, then the gate which accessed the runway was opened, and the passengers grabbed hold of their suitcases and went through the gate. I then realised that as most of the airport staff were on strike, passengers had to walk to the plane with their suitcases. This plane took off, and in the next four or five hours there were only about five planes. Mehrabad was usually a very busy airport, but since a lot of flights had been cancelled, plus the Government offices were closed, making it impossible to get an Exit Visa, this part of the airport was quiet! A stark contrast to the remainder of the airport.

As the following few flights arrived, which were practically empty, I started talking to the airline staff at the departure gates, asking how full the planes were leaving Tehran. The first four were full, but I found a flight which had a few seats left on it. I approached one of the staff on the gate this flight was departing from.

> "Is this flight fully booked? We are desperate to leave today", I enquired tentatively. Judi and Antony were told to look frightened and distressed, which under the circumstances this was not difficult.
>
> "Our flight has been cancelled", I added, "And we are stuck here with nowhere to go".
>
> "I'll see if we can help", responded the gate attendant.
>
> "I've got tickets", I added. The attendant disappeared into a small office by the flight gate, to reappear about five minutes

later.

"Where are your suitcases?", he asked, "Are they booked through on another flight?".

"No, we only have cabin bags", I replied. He disappeared in the office again, and shortly reappeared.

"For $100 each, you can have seats on the next flight, but no luggage except your hand baggage", he offered. I agreed, gave him $300 and showed him our tickets. He put the money in his pocket and didn't even look at our tickets!

I had negotiated a flight to Istanbul on Turkish Airlines!!

It was an uneventful flight to Istanbul on a plane which wasn't much more than half full. We arrived at Istanbul Ataturk airport about four hours later that same evening. I went to the Tourist Information kiosk at the airport and found a mid-priced hotel to stay in.

Once we reached our hotel, I contacted Mr. Zelkas and told him our situation. He said that he had arranged tickets for the three of us from London to Jeddah for the end of November. It was about ten days away, so we decided to have a week's holiday in Istanbul. Which we did!

Chapter Four

Saudi Arabia

Our week holiday in Istanbul was enjoyable, doing all the tourist things that one would expect to be doing.

We visited the Blue Mosque, Topkapi Palace, and the Grand Bazaar, where I'm certain we paid too much

for everything we bought, even though I thought myself a good negotiator! It was uneventful, which is what we wanted, and I had no problem booking airline tickets to take us back home to England.

Before leaving to go to Iran, we had decided to let our house, rather than sell it, just to make sure we didn't get left behind on the property market, and the rental income would help towards the mortgage payments. Consequently, we didn't have a home to go to, but this was not going to be a problem since we were only going to be in England for a few days.

Before arriving in London, I had contacted Mr. Zelcas from EDS. He had booked us a reasonable hotel, at EDS's expense, for us to stay in for the few days before we were due to fly out to Jeddah. Roger, an EDS representative was waiting to greet us at Heathrow when we arrived, and we were chauffeured to our hotel. London was cold and wet, as you would expect in November, but we had no car accidents on the way to the hotel!

"Here we are!", announced Roger as we stopped outside the hotel.

"Looks like a nice hotel", Judi commented. "This will be fine for the next three days".

"Thanks, Roger", said I, "What's the arrangements for our travel to Jeddah?"

> "The hotel and all your meals have been paid for by EDS, and here are your airline tickets. You don't need any Visas for Jeddah as they are arranged by the EDS staff when you get to Jeddah airport. There will be someone at the airport to meet you and get the administration sorted out."

I thanked Roger. He left, and we never saw him again.

I had the airline tickets in my hands for three seats on the Saudi Arabian Airlines flight to Jeddah, which was leaving in three days' time. A taxi had also been arranged to collect us from the hotel to take us to Heathrow airport.

The next few days was another mini-holiday. We had never holidayed in London before, and I had only been there a couple of times on business when I worked for IBM. We took in a few of the tourist spots, including the Tower of London, and enjoyed our leisure time there as a family. Antony was quite excited about it, as he had never been to London, and at eleven years old, he liked the Tower of London, and a fairly new gruesome attraction called The London Dungeon!

Those few days just flew over, and the morning came for us to leave. Taxi arrived, took us to Heathrow, we checked in (we had a couple of suitcases and some new clothes by now), and headed off to the departure gate. Everything was so relaxed, efficient, and civilized compared to Tehran. Our three seats were together, and we had an uneventful relaxed flight to Jeddah. I was not concerned that alcohol was not served, as we knew Saudi Arabia was a 'dry' country. The flight took about seven hours, but we were fed and watered well, and the time flew over as we anticipated our new World.

We touched down at Jeddah International Airport on time, and left the aircraft with the other passengers, emerging into a pleasantly warm late evening. We were all ushered to Passport Control, which seemed to run quite efficiently, if not slowly. We approached the uniformed Official sitting at the desk.

"Good evening", I said, wondering if he spoke English.

"Good evening to you also, and Welcome to Saudi Arabia", he responded pleasantly, in English, as I handed over our passports for inspection. He flipped through all three of them, then did the same again.

"Visas?", he questioned. "Where are your Visas?".

Beyond the Passport Control point I could see people milling about, and could see one guy holding up a large card with 'COVELLE' written on it.

"The guy over there has our Visas", I said to the Official, as I pointed him out.

"No Visa in your passport, no entry!" the now stern faced official insisted.

Two policemen approached us, one taking me by the arm, the other taking Judi and Antony, and walked us through the barrier to a small office, with a Customs Officer, where we were asked to sit.

I repeated to the Customs Officer that the guy outside was from EDS, and had our Visas. One of the policemen was sent out to fetch him. Within a few minutes two men came back with the policeman, the guy holding the card with our name on it, who was actually Pakistani, and an American who introduced himself as Ryan, who was the Country Manager for EDS Saudi Arabia.

"What's the problem?", I asked Ryan, after introducing myself, "Where are our Visas?"

Ryan looked rather embarrassed and replied,

"You should have your Entry Visas stamped in all your passports, plus a Work Visa in yours".

"I was told this would be done at the airport", I spluttered, "We don't have anything in our passports at all, so what happens now?"

"As a company, we have only recently started doing contracts in the Middle East", explained Ryan. "We have a contract here and another in Kuwait", he continued, "In Kuwait, we can get Entry Visas at the airport, but not in Saudi Arabia! I guess someone wasn't aware of this at Head Office back in the States!"

What happened next, was that we were deported!

As EDS were at fault, they paid for the return tickets for us to go back to London. If they had not paid, the Saudi Government would have paid for tickets to the closest country which would take us, which at that time would probably have been Turkey or The Yemen!

The next flight to London was the plane we had only just got off. It was being cleaned and refuelled, ready for departure in two hours. We sat in the office for about an hour, then we were escorted back to the plane by Security and sat back in the same three seats we had occupied on the flight from England. We were the first on the plane, and as the Security man handed me our passports he just said,

"Sorry!"

Whilst we were on our flight back to Heathrow, Ryan was organising someone to meet us and making arrangements for somewhere for us to stay back in London.

Upon our arrival at Heathrow, at about 7am, we were met at the airport by a representative from EDS. I didn't inquire about his name, nor did he offer it. We got in the car, and surprise, surprise, we were taken to the same hotel we had checked out of the day before. Just as well we didn't take any hotel towels with us!

The following morning the American guy who was in charge of the EDS office in the UK, Jayden, came to see us. Understandably, he was very apologetic, and told us that the Visa applications were going in that morning, and normally take a week to process, he believed. At that point I was made aware that I was the first 'Brit' they had ever employed, and not coming from the USA had caused some confusion. However, the hotel bill and all meals would be paid for by EDS, and so that we didn't get bored for the next week, EDS would give us £25 a day so we could visit the tourist attractions at their expense. I was also told that there was a small hitch with the University contract in Jeddah, and it was not starting until 10th December, and not the 1st December as was expected, but I would be on the payroll from 1st December. Time for another expenses paid holiday! So far, I was quite impressed with my treatment by EDS, if not with their efficiency.

A week passed, and Jayden came to see us.

> "Your Visa has come through, Jeff", he said, "but not Judi's and Antony's. Sometimes dependants take a week or two longer".
>
> "My contract is a 'married status' one", I reminded Jayden, "We all go together! It's less than three weeks to Christmas, and we always spend Christmas together as a family."
>
> "That won't be a problem", assured Jayden, "but you must be in Jeddah at contract start, or we lose the contract! Judi and Antony will be with you well before Christmas."
>
> "As long as we are together within a couple of weeks, I think we can handle that", I stated, and Judi nodded in agreement.

Jayden had the airline ticket for the next day, again, with Saudi Arabian Airlines, which he handed to me along with my passport, which I checked had both an Entry Visa and a Work Visa in it. It was a familiar procedure the next day, with the taxi to Heathrow, and the flight (not the same seat) to Jeddah. This time I walked confidently up to Customs and was allowed entry.

I was met by Ryan, who greeted me over enthusiastically, as one would a lost brother, and took me to my modern, newly furnished two bedroomed apartment, in the block rented by EDS for their Expat staff. There was food in the fridge, bedding on one of the beds, and I was told I would be collected the following morning to be taken to the EDS offices for 'Administrative Processing', where we could also have coffee and do-nuts!

The next morning, I went to the EDS office for a chat and do-nut with Ryan before one of the company drivers, Asim (the Pakistani guy from the airport), drove me to the Jeddah University to meet Don, the Account Manager. Don was American (not a surprise), in his late 50's, six feet tall, obviously used to play American Football, judging by his stature, had black close cropped thinning hair, and was rather brusk. He wore a dark blue suit, dark blue tie, white shirt, and black laced wingtip shoes.

We shook hands, but he seemed to view me with some disdain.

"We have a dress code here", he stated, "and your attire does not meet it!"

"Pardon!", was all I could think of to say.

I was dressed in one of the two new suites I had bought for my new job. This one was beige, the other a light grey. I also wore a cream shirt with a patterned tie, and beige leather slip on shoes.

"You will have to get a dark suit, dark tie, and black shoes", he continued.

"No dress code was mentioned to me", I responded, "and I think for the climate here, my clothes would actually seem to be a lot more suitable than yours! How much clothing allowance do you give for this 'uniform' EDS wants me to wear?"

"We don't provide an allowance, we just expect staff to wear what EDS tells them to wear, and the black shoes must be lace up wingtips!"

"Not a chance!", I retorted, "You buy my clothes, you might get a say in what they are! If the Customer complains to you about my dress sense, then I will change them, otherwise, forget it!"

"And another thing", Don continued, "EDS staff should be clean shaven!"

I had a full beard, as I had since I was seventeen years old, apart from when I was in the Territorial Army. EDS did not allow facial hair, except for a small moustache.

This was not a good start for my new job. I later found out that almost all of EDS was made up of ex-US Military personnel, who were obviously used to being told what to do, even down to their clothing. I was not. As a compromise, I said I would shave my beard, just to keep him happy, or at least as happy as he was ever going to get!

I reluctantly shaved my beard off the following day.

Don showed me my office at the University, luckily, he worked in the EDS office!

My official title was 'Computer Operations Manager' and I was introduced to my university boss, Mohammed, who was Saudi Arabian, and my Computer Operators and Programmers, who were all American, and all worked for EDS. I was already beginning to have doubts about my choice of employer.

The next two weeks was a steep learning curve for me, although one computer installation was much like any other. The next time I saw Mohammed, he actually said how much he liked my suit, commenting that he could not understand why all Westerners seemed to like dark clothing in such a hot climate! He wore a brilliant white Thobe (traditional Arabic garment), with pearl buttons and silver stitching. Mohammed was seldom seen, so I was quite autonomous in the way things were done, as long as the weekly report was on his desk. There was really not that much to do. Most processing was University Administration, with some test runs for budding computer programmers. The American computer operators were training the Saudi computer operators, and the same went for the computer programmers.

I spoke with Judi most evenings on the telephone. Quite a laborious affair, which involved booking a timeslot with the International Overseas Operator, which could end up being two hours later than booked, and lasted only fifteen minutes, at which time you were abruptly cut off. I checked progress on Judi's and Antony's Visa daily, and just told it was being processed. It was less than a week until Christmas when I went in to see Ryan about the Visas.

"Any progress on the Visas?", I chirped.

"I've heard nothing yet", replied Ryan.

"Sorry, not good enough!", was my response, "Do I need to remind you of my 'married status' contract, and what I was promised before I came here?"

"We are trying our best!", returned Ryan.

"Still not good enough, Ryan", I continued, "If Judi and Antony are not on the flight from London tomorrow, I want a ticket back to London to spend Christmas with them, or you can have my resignation".

Ryan was taken aback. He was not used to subordinates making demands!

Tomorrow came, but Judi and Antony didn't. I handed in my notice, which I had written, and was immediate, since EDS had broken our contract. I was in a position of power, as I knew EDS did not have anyone else who could carry out the Operations Manager roll, and they could easily lose the contract.

"Leave it with me for the day", Ryan requested, "We will definitely sort it out today!".

True to his word, Ryan did sort it out. I was given an airline ticket to Heathrow for the following day, and told I had ten days 'Christmas Holiday', in the UK, and would return with my family on the 2nd January. EDS would also continue to pay for the London hotel for this period. That made me a very, very, happy man!

We enjoyed our unexpected Christmas holiday in England. Did more London tourist stuff, and visited our friends Terry (him) and Paddy (her), who lived near Portsmouth, plus a few others who didn't live too far from London, as we didn't have a car.

EDS Administration was obviously busy over the Christmas period sorting out visas for us, and just before the New Year, Jayden turned up with our passports.

"Visa situation is all sorted out", he beamed. I looked at the passports, and there was an Entry Visa stamp in all three of them now.

"That's great", I responded, "Do you have the flights arranged?"

"Sure do. They are for the 2nd January", Jayden told us, "Same taxi routine as last time".

As expected, the taxi arrived on the arranged time, we flew to Jeddah again, with Saudi Arabian Airways, and again an uneventful flight.

At Customs all three of us stood quietly in the queue. Judi and I were both very apprehensive and my stomach had the flutters. We reached the front of the queue. The official looked at our passports, then turned to show them to another more senior official. They exchanged words. Judi looked worried. I believe I broke wind. The official then handed me back all three passports saying,

"Welcome to Saudi Arabia!"

We were in!

It was a short walk to collect our suitcases, and we were met there by Ryan and Asim. We were whisked off to our apartment, where we were left to unpack. Ryan took Judi's and Antony's passports with him back to the EDS office for 'processing'.

"Well, that's that all sorted", I thought to myself, but it wasn't!!

I was at work at the University the next day, while Judi and Antony were settling into their new home. Mid-morning, Asim turned up, telling me I needed to go back to the office with him. (One of Asim's duties was driving EDS staff from the EDS office to the EDS contract sites, if they did not have their own car, and also driving the ladies around to where-ever they wanted to go.) Back at the EDS offices Ryan beckoned me into his room.

"There is a problem with Judi and Antony's visas", he blurted out. "They are only 3-day visas, which we have applied to be upgraded to annual ones, but this type cannot be upgraded. We need a different type of visa!".

"So, what's the problem? Surely you can get this done at the Government Offices downtown within three days, can't you?", I said.

"No. We can't", continued Ryan, "The type of visa they need can only be issued in country of birth, so they have to go back to London!"

I was absolutely astounded. What the Hell am I doing working for a Mickey Mouse organisation like this! Was my old IBM manager right! I made my feelings known. After I had calmed down, Ryan told me that the flights would be arranged for the next day for Judi and Antony to return, again, to London, where accommodation would be provided for the couple of days they would be there. I would have to stay in Jeddah because I had already been away from the University contract for as long as I had been there.

When I returned to the apartment to break the news to Judi, it did not go down well, but she agreed to return to the UK with Antony. I saw the two of them off at the airport the following day, expecting them back a few days later, but things didn't happen quite that quickly!

On Judi and Antony's arrival at Heathrow, they were again greeted by an EDS representative, who took them to a hotel on the Tottenham Court Road, which was to be their home for the next couple of days. Unfortunately, the visa took a lot longer than two days, the Saudi Embassy saying it would take two weeks. Judi and Antony left the hotel after about a week and went to stay with our friends Terry and Paddy in Portsmouth. It was over three weeks before EDS received the visas, which were actually only for a 24 hour stay in Saudi Arabia, but could be upgraded, I was told!

At least Judi and Antony were with friends, and I was still able to phone them every other day.

While my family were in England, my work at the University continued as normal, and I was already starting to get a bit bored with it.

During this time, I decided I wanted my beard back because I felt naked without it, and I got a rash when I shaved. Through one of the British Expat Clubs I'd heard about, I managed to find a British doctor who was practising in Jeddah. I made an appointment to see him, showed him the rash on my face, told him about the 'rules' my employer had, and asked his opinion.

> "Absolutely ridiculous", he said, "An infringement of personal liberties, and most of the Arabs have beards anyway!".

He then wrote me a letter to present to EDS saying I couldn't shave because of medical reasons! I presented the letter to Don the next day. He wasn't happy about it, but said nothing. That was the last day I shaved in Saudi Arabia!

I got on fine with most of the EDS staff, and became very friendly with Fred and Judy, who were, of course American. A few days after Judi and Antony left, I decided I needed my own transport, and somebody knew somebody who had a car for sale, so I bought it. It was a one year old Toyota Corona, and gave me the freedom to go shopping when I wanted, do a bit of exploring around the city, and not rely on the rather unreliable Asim.

The second weekend I was in Jeddah I was invited to join Fred and Judy at the beach for the day with a few of the other EDS staff. We headed to a local beach about an hour out of town, and I took my 'new' car for its first trip out of town. Jeddah ended very abruptly in 1979. About five miles from where we lived, the surfaced road just stopped, and became a wide dirt track. After travelling along this track for about half an hour, we took a sharp right onto a narrow sandy track, which went to the 'beach'. Obviously, this was a well used track, as it was corrugated. It was at this point that I realised that a Toyota Corona saloon car was not the car I needed.

The car literally started to fall apart! The rear view mirror dropped off, one of the sun visors fell off, and the trim around the glove compartment fell off. I also managed to lose one of the wheel trims. When we arrived at the beach fifteen minutes later, I thought my teeth were going to fall out.

The beach was called seventeen palms, but there were actually ten, two halves, and the rest were stumps.

We pulled up at a quiet spot (which was almost anywhere), and I jumped out of my car with the bits that had fallen off in my hand.

"Look what has happened to my new car", I spurted out to Fred, "I've only had it a week!"

"It's because it's new", Fred explained.

"What do you mean, because it's new?", I returned.

"All the bits fall off after a few trips to the beach", said Fred, "It happens to them all! My Datsun is two years old, and everything that can fall off, already has."

At that point I decided I needed an off-road vehicle as I thought I would like to explore the countryside and beaches at some length.

Fred and Judy had brought a picnic for the three of us. I did like Judy, but she had a lot of trouble understanding me. She was from a small town in Ohio, I am from the North-East of England! We had chicken. Judy offered me a chicken breast on a plate.

"Have you any salt?", I asked.

"Excuse me", responded Judy.

"I'd like some salt", said I. Judy handed me a fork.

"Salt, please", I repeated. Judy looked puzzled and handed me a napkin.

"Do you have salt?", I said very slowly. Judy handed me a knife, saying,

"I can't quite catch what you are saying."

I rummaged around the picnic basket and found some salt. I held it up and we all started laughing. I was actually the first English person Judy had met, and she thought everyone in England spoke like the Queen.

It was a beautiful sunny day and we swam in the sea and lazed on the beach until late afternoon, before heading home. Several other bits fell off my car on the way back.

I asked around as to what was the best way to buy an off-road vehicle. I was told there was an area in Jeddah which was where all the new and used car dealers were, but the new vehicles were more than I wanted to spend, and I was told the used car dealers would rip me off, as I was a Westerner. I was then told to have a look on the Supermarket notice boards, as that was where all the Expats bought and sold everything.

My spare time for the next two weeks was spent scouring the supermarket notice boards, as I wanted to have a decent vehicle to take Judi and Antony to the beach when they arrived in Jeddah. I found one for sale, which looked just the job. It was a Chevrolet Blazer, which is a large American 4-wheel drive truck, with an eight-cylinder 5.7 litre engine. The guy who was selling it was an English guy called Stuart. I telephoned him.

"I believe you have a Chevy Blazer for sale", I enquired, "I'm interested, but don't know how to find you".

"Great", replied Stuart, "I'll bring it round for you to see to-morrow. Where do you work?".

I told him I was at the University, and he brought the Chevy round the next afternoon. When he turned up, it was like looking at me with spectacles! We could easily have been taken for brothers. We were both the same weight, at fifteen stone, give or take a pound or two; we were both 5'11", both quite heavily built, and we both had closely cropped black hair and a full beard. Stuart wore spectacles, which I didn't. Stuart had already worked in Jeddah for about two years, and was in charge of a company which did swimming pool maintenance.

We immediately liked each other, and I bought his yellow Chevy

Blazer. He was buying a much newer one of the same type and make. He also invited me round to his apartment for dinner, and to meet his wife, Jenny. We are still friends to this day! I told Stuart I was keen on doing some off-roading, and he invited Judi and I to come along on his next trip out, which was in a couple of weeks' time. He even brought my new truck round to my apartment the next day, and told me he knew someone who would be interested in buying my Toyota, which he did two days later for the same price I had bought it for!

At last, the visas for Judi and Antony were issued by the Saudi Embassy in London. It had taken over four weeks and the visas were for 24-hours only!

I was a bit sceptical.

However, they were booked on the usual flight, arrived at the usual time, and joined the usual queue at Customs and Immigration. I was at the airport waiting with Ryan, Asim, and a small, portly Arab man. Judi and Antony were in the queue, and approaching the Customs Official at the desk. Just before they reached the desk, the little Arab man went up to the control gate, showed the policeman standing there a pass of some sort, and just joined Judi and Antony at the desk. The Customs Official had taken Judi and Antony's passports and was discussing the visas with another Official. The small Arab man interrupted their conversation whilst brandishing his pass and a single sheet of paper. He pointed at the paper and a heated discussion took place.

> "Not again!", I said to myself, then the same to Ryan. "You told me that the visas had been issued and approved! There seems to be a problem, I think!".
>
> "Not a problem.", responded Ryan, "The letter is signed by our Saudi Sponsor, who is a Prince, and the little Arab guy is the person who sorts out these kinds of issues for the Prince."

I still wasn't convinced, but after a five-minute raised voice discussion, Judi and Antony were allowed through. At Last! Immediately they were through the Arrivals gate, the little Arab guy took the passports, and rushed off.

"Where is he going with those passports?" I asked Ryan.

"To the Prince, then tomorrow to the Government offices. He has 24 hours to get them upgraded to annual dependants' visas", was Ryan's response. "There won't be any problems, it's just costing us a lot of money!"

The five of us got into Ryan's American car, and he took us back to our apartment. It seems Asim was not there in his role as a driver that day, but as an interpreter, should we have needed one.

Judi was impressed with the apartment, but not with where it was, which looked like the middle of a building site, but as I pointed out, Jeddah was a building site!

In 1979 the amount of construction which was taking place in the city was phenomenal. Judi had seen the apartment briefly on her previous short visit, but was too traumatised to really take it in. The only thing missing in our apartment was our shipment of personal items, which had still not arrived from Tehran, but they did arrive two weeks later, after taking three weeks to clear Customs!

Two days later Judi's and Antony's passports were delivered to the EDS office with the correct visas in them.

We were ready to start our Saudi Arabian adventure.

Over the next couple of weeks Judi and Antony got to know the rest of the EDS staff, and I took them round to meet Stuart and Jenny. Judi and Jenny immediately bonded, and Judi also liked Stuart very much.

Stuart and Jenny also had a daughter about the same age as Antony, but she was at school in England.

As it was early February, the School Year had recently started. A place in the local school had been reserved for Antony, so he started almost immediately. The school was called the Parents Cooperative School, and had been founded in the mid 1950's for the children of Expats. The only problem for us, was that it had an American curriculum.

On the week-end (Thursday and Friday, again!), we went down the same beach I went to a few weeks before, but this time in our Chevy Blazer. Definitely the right car for the job. The heavy-duty suspension just skimmed over the corrugations, and although there was plenty of rattling, nothing fell off!

We went with Stuart and Jenny, and Fred and Judy also came with us.

Jenny was a slender lady of about 5'6", with short curly light brown hair, she had very sharp facial features, particularly her nose, and a terrible temper once she got upset. Completely different to my Judi and Judy, who were both 5'7" and quite heavily built. Both had shoulder length dark brown hair, although Judy had a much more rounded face than Judi. Fred was only about 5'6" tall, and of an average build. He had black hair, with a bushy moustache, and was always smiling. Like most of the EDS employees, he was ex-Military, and had been trained as a computer programmer by EDS.

We enjoyed our time at the beach, and Antony loved swimming above the reef, which dropped straight down from about five feet to fifty feet!

The only drawback with this area of beach was that it was well used, by a lot of the Ex-Pat community and the locals, so it was not very private, and not really the place you would want to stay overnight. For this it was necessary to travel another hour out of Jeddah, and involved driving for an hour across the desert. This was desert without any tracks!

Two weeks later we tried the 'new' beach, where we stayed overnight. This beach was only accessible with a four-wheel drive vehicle, so Fred and Judy didn't come with us. Harvey, an American friend of Stuart and Jenny came with his wife Gale. Harvey was from Texas, and looked it. Medium height, brown hair, a moustache, and blue eyes. Always wore a Stetson hat! His wife was small, about 5'2", slightly built, dark complexion and hair, and looked very Mexican. Their four-wheel drive vehicle was a Nissan Patrol.

Antony was keen to try dune riding on a motorcycle, so we bought him a small Honda DAX70, which of course we all tried.

> "Can I go in the dunes, Dad?", Antony asked as soon as we arrived at our overnight camp site on the deserted Beach.
>
> "Of course, Just don't go too far from the beach", I replied, and off he went. He was in sight all of the time, but he was having problems getting up the sand dunes.
>
> "Bring the bike back here", I shouted across the sands, "Let Stuart show us how it's done".

Stuart showed us, but actually, he wasn't as good as Antony! Then I had a go and Harvey had a go, and then we came to the conclusion that the wheels on the bike were too small, so we just bombed up and down the deserted beach, and occasionally let Antony have a go!

I was also keen to have a go at windsurfing, so I had bought a second-hand windsurfer which we had also brought with us. As our Blazer was a large vehicle, we could fit the three of us inside with the motorcycle, but it was not ideal. The windsurfer fitted comfortably on the roof.

The following week I had a rack fitted to the back bumper of the Blazer, so we could carry the bike on it.

Judi and I also had a pleasant surprise that evening while we were having our BBQ on the beach. (Not too sophisticated, just a shallow hole in the sand lined with tin foil, a few BBQ briquettes, and an open grill tray from an oven on the top.) Both Stuart and Harvey had brought some alcohol with them! Saudi Arabia is a 'dry' country and the sale or consumption of alcohol is illegal. Stuart had brought a bottle of the local illegally brewed spirit, called Siddique (Arabic for 'my friend'), and Harvey had some of his home-made wine.

Harvey brewed a good red wine, and the siddique was a good

gin substitute when mixed with tonic water, or vodka substitute mixed with 7-Up! We all got quite merry.

We returned home on Friday evening, after a thoroughly enjoyable weekend. We would certainly be doing this again.

Over the next months we went out on several trips, but never more than a couple of days each. We used the 'local' holidays to explore the local desert regions and the Red Sea coastline.

Things continued uneventfully, and a bit boring at work, for about four months, then three things happened at once.

At work, EDS had secured a second contract, which was to provide computing services for the construction of the new airport which was just starting to be built. Basically, the EDS contract was for the development and running of a centralised computer system to provide computer resources for the many contractors on the airport, control all of the project finances for the airport project planners, support the computer hardware and software, and train Saudi Arabian Nationals in all aspects of the computer systems.

The bit which I was especially interested in, was the requirement for two hundred remote computer terminals spread across the new airport construction site. The contract specifically called for a Computer Communications Manager. That was a job I wanted! I popped into the office to see Ryan one morning.

"I hear EDS have won the new Jeddah International Airport computing services contract", was my opening comment.

"Yes, we have", confirmed Ryan, "Now I need to get some staff for it pretty quickly. The contract starts next month! These bloody Salesmen promise the Earth, then expect me to deliver it!".

"How about a Comms Manager? Do you have anyone for the position yet?", I enquired.

"Nothing at all. We've had no response from our US or UK Recruitment Agencies. They can get us an Operations Manager, Computer Operators, Systems Programmers, and Application Programmers, but no Comms guys".

"Just a suggestion", I ventured, "but my background is really in Data Communications, and I'd like to set-up this network from scratch, if you can get an Operations Manager for the University project".

Ryan's face lit up.

"That would be great! You can start at the airport site as soon as the contract is signed, and I'll get a replacement for you for the University."

We were both happy, and I was to remain on the airport project for the next five years! Also, Don was no longer my boss!

The second thing that happened was Judi getting a part time job at the PCS school, the school Antony was attending, as an Administrative Assistant. Judi was getting a little bored at the apartment, even though she was making friends, and the EDS driver would take her anywhere she wanted to go, as long as she sat in the back seat of the car. Women were not allowed to drive in Saudi Arabia, and could not sit beside someone in the car who they were not related to!

Judi enjoyed the work, which was doing a bit of typing, filing, and helping out in the library. She told me of her first day in the library, which apart from being where pupils borrowed books, was also the place where the boxes of new school books were delivered to. A shipment arrived.

"These need to be checked over", the Librarian told Judi, "They are Atlases".

"How do I check an Atlas?", responded Judi.

"Well," said the Librarian, "by check, I actually mean censor".

"How do you censor an Atlas?", questioned Judi.

"I'll show you on the first one". replied the Librarian.

The Librarian took the first of the two hundred Atlases out of the carton, turned to the page which showed the Middle East, and with a thick black marker pen, totally blacked out 'Israel'!

> "Israel does not exist according to Saudi Arabia!", she told Judi.

Judi spent the rest of the day removing Israel from the World!

The third thing that happened was the realisation that the PCS American school would not be suitable for Antony for the upcoming and subsequent years. Judi and I wanted Antony to have a good English education, and English qualifications. We decided, although Antony was not happy about it, to have Antony educated in a private residential school in England. As I was due two weeks holiday leave in a couple of weeks, we decided to have one week in Greece, followed by one week in England to sort out a school for Antony.

We immediately sent off for details for several UK schools which we had been recommended, by either British Expats or the British Consulate. I was quite taken aback by the cost of residential schooling, as it would cost about 65% of my salary. My salary was £9,000, the school fees were almost £6,000!

I approached Ryan about this.

> "Hi Ryan, I've got a problem I think you can help me with", was my opening gambit. "It could affect my position at the Airport project".

> "What's that, Jeff? I'm always here to help where I can, and we do need you for this project!", was Ryan's response.

I hinted that I may have to leave EDS for a better paid job, or return to the UK to work because of the schooling problem I had with Antony. As he also had a son of school age, he understood my position. I said how expensive the school would be, and was about to suggest that EDS could pay me the PCS school fees of about £3,000, which EDS were paying, and that would go towards the British school fees. I would then only have about half of the fees to pay myself. I was then going to ask for a salary increase to further help offset the cost of Antony's education. Before I had a chance to open my mouth, Ryan continued,

> "We think that families come first in EDS, and as long as we can keep you happy, we know you will give us 100% effort in your work. EDS will pay Antony's school fees, on presentation of the school's invoice for each term. We will also pay for a return ticket from the UK to Saudi Arabia at the end of each term, should he want to come here, and I can add that to your Contract, now!"

I almost fell over! Best negotiated outcome I've ever had, and I didn't even have to negotiate!

We had our holiday in Athens, then went to England and looked at several schools. We ended up with a shortlist of three, from which we let Antony pick the one he would prefer to attend. He was quite excited about going to an English residential school, but still would have preferred to stay with us in Jeddah. However, three months was the longest time he would be in England without us, and Judi and I also spent some of our vacation time back in England. Antony, now in his 50's, still thinks this was not a good idea, insisting he hated his time at school in England, but I contend that it definitely was a good choice.

Antony is now a determined achiever, which he was not, before his boarding school days.

Antony started his new school in September 1980, and Judi and I returned to Saudi. Antony would be joining us again in Jeddah in mid-December.

On our return to Jeddah, I started my new job at the airport. 'Airport' was probably not the correct term. It was actually a vast lump of desert about twenty miles north of the city, with a fence around it! It had several temporary buildings spread about the forty square mile site, the largest one being the Administration Centre, the remainder were those of the various contractors involved in the construction of what was going to be the largest airport in the World. It was a five-year project.

On my first day I was introduced to my new boss, and the few EDS staff who were already there. My new boss was an Arab, Prince Waleed, who had been educated at Eton in England. His English was probably better than mine. He was very affable, but knew absolutely nothing about computing. My new job was, to my surprise, Computer Operations Manager, as well! It seemed that the Communication Manager position would report to the Director of Computer Operations, the same as the Computer Operations Manager, who wasn't appointed yet, so it was me on a temporary basis. No problem, I was in very familiar territory. In the set-up here there would be separate Comms staff and Ops staff, reporting to different managers, with Prince Waleed (Director of Computer Operations) in charge of both, and the programming and system programming staff being part of Operations.

There would, of course, be Saudi Arabian trainees in all areas.

The computer had just been installed by IBM, and was still in the 'Acceptance' phase, so nothing was actually running live. The systems and development programmers had started their work, which had been defined by the Systems Analysts. All quite standard.

Basically, not much to do yet, other than oversea the programmers on EDS's behalf. I was given an indication as to where the various computer terminals were to be located. It was a mammoth task. Two hundred computer terminals spread over a forty square mile desert site linked into a single mainframe computer. Looked like I was going to have a great, if not challenging, time.

At this time, I decided I would like to meet the creatures of the Red Sea in their environment, so I decided to learn to Scuba dive. There was only one dive school in Jeddah at that time, and it was run by two Americans to the American PADI accreditation standard. I enjoyed my twelve-lesson training course in early 1980, which gave me my basic 'Open Water Diver' accreditation, which was all I wanted. Some of the training was a little scary.

> "Expect the unexpected", is what Ron, my tutor kept telling me, "Stay alert and don't panic".

After three or four lessons in a swimming pool, where we had to prove we were competent swimmers, knew how to communicate under water, and handle emergency situations, we were taken down to a quiet bit of breach where the reef was about twenty down, then dropped vertically for about another forty feet. Up to this point we had never been deeper than ten feet. At twenty feet we swam around and Ron and his colleague were pulling our masks off, pulling our mouthpieces out, and turning off our air supplies. We did our 'buddy breathing', where we shared one mouthpiece, and had to remove our scuba tanks and squeeze through tight spaces holding the tank.

By far the scariest part for me was the 'free ascent'. This involved going down to a depth of sixty feet, which was about twice that of normal sport diving, and swimming to the surface on one gulp of air! Something I thought I could never do, as it takes a minimum of two minutes, and it is necessary to breath out all of the time. Of course, the air expands in the lungs as you ascend, and the first thing you do on breaking the surface is actually breath out, not in!

After the twelve lessons I got my dive diploma, in June 1980, and I was ready to go.

If we did not go to the desert trekking on weekends, I would always go scuba diving with one of my dive buddies, and often in the evening during the week.

It was on one of our drives to one of my favourite diving sites with my dive buddy, Dave, that I had my only encounter with the Saudi traffic police. We were well outside of the city limits, where the speed limit was 130kph. The roads were unmade, that is, not tarmacked, and just dusty tracks. We were travelling at about 100kph and overtook a police car with the dust billowing up as we passed. We were only a few hundred meters past the police car when I heard his siren and saw his orange lights flashing behind me. I thought he must be on his way to an incident, so I slowed down to let him pass. To my surprise, he waved me down.

The two officers got out of the car and walked over to me.

"You are speeding!" said one in faltering English.

"I don't think so," I responded, "I was only doing 100kph, and the speed limit is 130kph."

"You ARE speeding." He repeated more forcefully. "You are driving too fast!"

"No, I wasn't!", I insisted.

"You were, all the dirt came in my window." He explained.

Unfortunately, the policeman had his car window open! He wasn't happy about the dust blowing in as we drove past, and decided to stop us for speeding. He didn't bother asking for my driver's licence, but just wrote out a speeding ticket and gave it to me.

"Both get out of the car." He said, and his partner got into the driver's seat of my car.

"What are you doing?" I asked.

"You get your car back when you have paid the fine."

We were left standing at the side of the road as we watched my car and the police car drive off. This was 1980. The first commercial mobile phone came out in 1983. We would have had to wait a long time to contact someone from where we were!

We managed to get a lift back into Jeddah in the back of a van carrying melons, where we found a public phone box and I called the EDS office, who sent their driver to pick us up.

The next step was to go and pay the fine, which was done at the police station in the city centre. After paying the fine, which was the equivalent of about £15, the next task was to collect my car. The confiscated cars were parked in one of two pounds, but nobody knew which one, so it was just luck if you got the right one first time.

I was advised by the EDS Saudi driver to collect our car as soon as possible, as the car parking in the car pound was not controlled in any way, so the longer you waited the more difficult it was to get your car out.

We were lucky, and my car was in the first pound we visited. One of the problems encountered when we arrived there was actually finding my car keys! There were probably five hundred cars in the pound, and all the keys were just thrown into an oil drum. It was up to you to find yours. I showed the receipt for my fine payment to the officer in charge, and was then given permission to rummage through the oil drum for my keys. Fortunately, they were quite close to the top.

The next challenge was to get my car out of the pound. Cars were just parked in concentric circles almost touching each other, so the longer your car had been there, the further towards the centre it would be. If your car had been there several weeks, many cars would be blocking it in, and then you had to rummage through the keys in the oil drum to find the keys of the cars you needed to move to get yours out!

Some cars had been there for months, and probably just abandoned by the owners for one reason or other. My car, which had been there less than a day was in the outer circle, so was relatively easy to get out.

This was quite an experience, and I never overtook a police car again!

I soon realised that the airport project was a bit limited for facilities, the main one being the lack of a restaurant. There was a tea room where you could make your own coffee and tea, but that was all there was apart from a microwave oven. Obviously, if you wanted to eat, you had to bring food with you from home. However, within a few days, I discovered there was a sandwich man.

He had a little trolley with an assortment of sandwiches, which he pushed along the corridors. He was a Pakistani who spoke no English at all. I selected my sandwich by looking at them. Over the first week I tried all of the different ones he had to offer, and decided one was really tasty. Just what I liked, definitely had some spices and chilli in it.

I settled on this one as my regular lunchtime snack for almost every day for the first month I was there.

I decided I liked it so much I would like to replicate it at home, if I could, but I needed to know what was in it. I asked Mohammed, one of the Arabic trainee computer operators to come with me when I was going for my next lunch sandwich, and ask the Pakistani guy what was in it.

> "Hello", said Mohammed (in Arabic) to the Pakistani guy, "My friend wants to know what you put in the sandwiches he likes", he continued.
>
> "Chilli mukh", responded the sandwich vendor.
>
> "I can guess what chilli is, but what is mukh?", I asked Mohammed. Mohammed's English was not too good, and he just pointed at his head, which I assumed meant he didn't know. He took me down the corridor to where his trainee programmer friend was working, and explained to him what was happening. His friend, who spoke very good English, just grinned at me and said.
>
> "Brains!"

It seems my favourite sandwich was mashed goat brains and chilli! I thought it would put me off, but I continued eating these sandwiches for a couple of years, until the airport staff cafeteria was built.

IBM handed the commissioned computer over to the Airport Project, and the basic installation of the customised application programs started. Most of the payrolls for the Saudi staff were processed on this computer, together with all of the project planning for the multitude of contract companies. There were dozens of foreign companies developing all of the ancillary systems needed to commission and run an airport. These contractors were spread all over the airport site, and it was my job to ensure they had computer terminals in their offices which could communicate with the IBM Mainframe computer.

Within a few months I had a staff of three data communications technicians, by which time I had installed the computer terminals in the administration block, and had started cable installation to some of the nearby buildings.

It actually took over a year to install computer terminals to all of the locations needed, as new locations were coming on-line all of the time.

Terminals which could not be 'locally' attached, that is more than one mile away from the IBM mainframe, had to be remotely attached using modems. Unfortunately, there was no telephone network installed yet, other than within the administration building, so microwave dishes were used. These were not very reliable, as the heat of the day tended to distort the microwave transmissions. We made do with this until the telephone company (another contractor) installed the telephone network on the airport site. The first two years were very busy for me, but since I was doing a good job, I was definitely in a good position to negotiate my annual financial package!

Judi had found a job! Although it was illegal for women to work in Saudi, she had got herself a job! She was talking to one of the American ladies, Susan, who she had become friendly with, and this lady was telling Judi that her husband, Charles, was complaining all the time about the standard of typing of the reports he was doing for his company, which was involved with mapping for the Saudi Arabian Government. He worked for the United States Geological Survey (USGS). The only typists they could get were male, and they were either Pakistani or Filipino, and English was a second language to them, and consequently, there were many errors in the typed documents. Judi was a secretary in the UK before we left to go to Iran, and also kept her skills up whilst in Iran.

USGS paid her too much for the work she did, and also sent a driver to pick her up for work. She worked three days a week, and enjoyed every moment of it. The only problem was that foreign companies were sometimes raided by the police, who obviously knew this was happening, and she had to hide in a basement room if this happened. USGS always managed to get a tip off if a raid was imminent!

Judi and I only lived in the EDS apartments for about a year. They were temporary accommodation whilst ESD were having their own 'compound' built. It was a bit of desert with a fence round it and security gates. The compound consisted of about forty detached two and three bedroom timber-frame constructed bungalows, a Recreational Centre, and a swimming pool. Some people didn't like it, but the majority did, including us. There was a lot more privacy, and we could have an illegal alcoholic drink sitting around the pool, or have a party in the recreational centre. When I lived in England, I used to make my own wine, and everything to do this was available in Saudi. I made good wine, even if I do say so myself!

Shortly after we moved into the new EDS compound there was a knock on the door one evening. It was answered by Judi. Edward, the seven-year-old boy from next door was standing there with something cupped in his hands.

> "Look what I've found." He said opening his cupped hands. It was a very small kitten, probably only two weeks old. "The mother was run over, and she had four kittens. I've found homes for three, but no-one wants this one. Will you take it?"

I don't much like cats, and Judi knew that, but Judi was really sorry for the kitten, and so I agreed we would take it, on condition that Judi would feed it every four hours it needed feeding, for the next month or so, which she did. Our kitten, who Judi named Fluffy, was fed milk, which she drank through the finger of a rubber glove with a hole in it.

Fluffy was a feral cat, and was vicious with everyone except us. She was definitely a good 'guard cat', not letting anyone into the house. Fluffy accompanied us on all our dessert trips, and came back to England with us, and lived to the age of eighteen.

Another good thing about living in the EDS compound was the different people we met, as about half of the houses were rented to two other American companies who were based in Jeddah.

Away from work Judi and I were enjoying the social life, and we both really enjoyed our 'expeditions' into to Saudi Arabian countryside.

As we were extending our trips further away from Jeddah, we decided we would try and get some sort of official sanctioning, as we were getting stopped by the police every fifty miles or so and being cross-examined about what we were doing!

Another minor problem was Stuart and Jenny's dogs. They had two Red Setters, and dogs were frowned upon by the locals in Saudi, and they were always an issue when we were stopped by the police. The only dogs officially allowed in Saudi Arabia were Salukis, which were hunting dogs used by the nomadic Bedouin.

Stuart had come up with a solution to this problem. He had made a very official looking passport for each of the dogs, complete with a photograph of each dog, and the breed was listed as 'English Saluki'. The passport was in English and Arabic. I don't think he would have gotten away with it if they were Poodles!

We decided to form the 'Saudi Arabian Natural History Society', and Stuart knew a Prince who would back us, as it was then a 'Cultural' pursuit. We would also have an Official Letter, signed by a Prince!

One of our first longer trips was with Stuart and Jenny, and Simon and Sal. I met Simon, who worked for one of the contractors at the airport, shortly after I started there. He was new to Saudi Arabia, wanted to explore, and had bought a four-wheel drive truck, an 'International Harvester', another American vehicle.

Simon was tall, over six feet, and very thin. He had light brown hair almost to shoulder length, thinning on top, and a long bushy beard. Sal was also tall and thin, being about 5'10" in height. She had gingery-brown short curly hair.

We took advantage of a local holiday tagged onto the weekend, so we had four days. We decided to visit a place called Medain Saleh, which I'd never heard of, but Stuart was aware of. It was quite a drive, being about 500 miles north from Jeddah. The roads in Saudi Arabia in the early 1980's were not good, and Medain Saleh was not even on a road! We set off early in the morning and headed north along the coastal road to Al Wajh, which was about 400 miles away, arriving there at about 2pm. We then did a sharp right turn into the desert on a little used Bedouin track, and just headed east. It was about another hundred miles to Medain Saleh, but we stopped after four hours, when we had driven another seventy miles, and set up camp in the desert for the night. We had a good evening with a BBQ, and chatted well into the late evening.

As usual Judi and I slept in the back of our Blazer. With the rear seats folded down and the tailgate down, there was just enough room for a double mattress, so it was a very sound, comfortable night's sleep.

Simon and Sal also slept in their truck, but it was not quite as comfortable, as it was narrower than ours, but they were quite thin anyway! Stuart and Jenny had a frame tent which they shared with their dogs.

We were up and away by about 10am the following morning, and covered the remaining twenty-five miles in about two hours. It was slow going as there wasn't much of a track, and the soft sand was quite deep. All low gear, low ratio, 4-wheel drive work. We had managed to fill up with fuel just before turning off into the desert, so with a twenty-five-gallon petrol tank, and three five-gallon jerry cans each, we didn't have to worry about fuel. Just as well, as our vehicles were getting less than five miles to the gallon in this terrain.

Medain Saleh just sort of appeared in front of us without warning. There were clumps of large rocks with elaborate carvings on one side, which was an entrance to the carved out interior of the rock. Some were individual, others looked like a row of terraced houses, and this was just on the outskirts of the site.

We stopped at the first tomb. Suddenly, there was someone standing beside us. He was obviously a guard or security guy of some sort. He was a rather scruffy looking dark skinned, bearded Arab without any uniform, but what was most obvious were the two bandoliers of gun cartridges, one strung across each shoulder. However, he was not carrying any sort of firearm, only a huge dagger in a scabbard at his waist. He placed one hand on his dagger and gestured us to follow him with his other. We walked for five minutes up to a small wooden shed, which was his office. The guard started talking rapidly in Arabic, and although Stuart could speak a little Arabic, he could only manage to make out that we shouldn't be here as it was a restricted Government location. We showed our piece of paper signed by the Prince, which was eventually accepted, although begrudgingly, and he said we could look around as long as he came with us.

We spent the rest of the afternoon looking around, although the guard seemed to get fed up after about an hour, and just disappeared.

We decided to set up our camp a few miles away from the site and return the next morning for a leisurely look around, as there seemed to be dozens of these tombs carved out of the rock.

From research which I later carried out, I discovered that these tombs were constructed by the same people, the Nabateans, who carved the tombs at Petra in Jordan, which is about 220 miles north-east of Medain Saleh. Both places were on the spice trade route in about the first century after Christ, and the Nabatean

Empire controlled this route.

The next morning, we returned and were greeted in a quite friendly manner by the guard, who again, just seemed to appear out of nowhere. He didn't want to see our letter this time, and obviously remembered us. We assumed he lived in the little wooden hut which was his 'office'.

By getting him to speak very slowly, Stuart was able to discover that not very many people had actually been here, and this area was only accessible with a special permit. (It seems a Prince's signature on a piece of paper constitutes a special permit in our case.) The guard told us there had been only three groups who had been to view the tombs in the previous six months, and all were foreigners!

He left us to our own devices, and we drove and walked around much of the area where the tombs were. We thought that there must have been about fifty of these carved rock tombs, but we later found out that there were well over a hundred.

There had been no effort to preserve or control access to these tombs and we found what we believe were fragments of human bones on some of the 'shelves' which were cut out of the rock inside of the tombs. We also found fragments of pottery and more bits of bone if we just scratched at the sandy floor of some of the tombs. We respectfully replaced anything we uncovered, taking nothing from the site. It was quite an experience! We left mid-afternoon and drove for about four hours, where we camped about a two-hour drive from Al Wajh. The next day was an easy uneventful drive home to Jeddah.

The tombs at Medain Saleh became Saudi Arabia's first World Heritage Site in 2008, twenty-eight years after we had visited it!

Later during 1980, when Antony had joined us during his summer break from school, he decided he would like to learn to scuba dive. He was already a strong swimmer for a thirteen year old and took to it like a duck to water. For the next four years he was my dive buddy whenever he was with us in Jeddah.

While Antony was with us, I decided to organise one of our 'Saudi Arabian Natural History Society' trips.

I had never actually led a trip before, although by now I was getting to be a pretty good dessert driver, so I decided to organise a trip to Al Waba.

Al Waba was a crater of some sort in the middle of the desert, but no one we knew had ever been there, and no one knew exactly where it was! I was told by some of the local Saudis, that it was where a meteor had landed, and others said it was an extinct volcano. I later found out that it was believed to have been caused by a meteor strike until the 1960s, but then it was proven to have been caused by volcanic activity underground. Magma coming into contact with underground water had caused the surface of the earth to explode, causing the crater.

I was talking to Stuart one day,

> "What do you think about going to Al Waba in a couple of weeks' time? There's a Public Holiday coming up, so we will have a long weekend." I said.
>
> "Do you know the way?", enquired Stuart.
>
> "No, but I can get a copy of a map of the area from one of the American guys who works at USGS (United States Geological Survey), it will show on there", I responded, "and we can ask Harvey and Gale if they want to join us".

Stuart agreed, so we would have three vehicles, and there would be eight of us, including Antony, and Stuart and Jenny's daughter, Andria, who was also in Jeddah for the school holidays.

Judi and I got on well with Charles and Susan, a couple of Americans from the USGS, and he had offered to copy a few maps for me before. He had no problem rummaging out one of the area for me. The maps were actually blown-up copies of aerial photographs. Charles and Susan asked us round to their house for dinner, and to give me the map.

"Here is the map you wanted", Charles said, as he handed me

a piece of photographic paper the size of a sheet of newspaper. I looked at it and noticed faint lines criss-crossing the whole map.

"What are the lines?", I enquired.

"They are the known tracks across the desert, where there aren't any roads", Charles replied.

"And are the numbers written on each track a sort of road number, and what does VPY mean by each number?", I asked.

"No", returned Charles, "They don't have any numbered tracks, and VPY stands for Vehicles Per Year!"

I was quite taken aback. The numbers ranged from two, up to the mid-sixties. This meant that the busy 'roads' would only have about one vehicle a week, and some only one vehicle every six months! Our chances of meeting other traffic on the off-road part of our journey was going to be pretty unlikely.

A week after getting the map we set off. As we weren't too sure where Al Waba was, I thought we had better take a compass and just follow a bearing once we had turned off the closest main road to where we thought it was. Luckily, I had a compass. I had gotten it out of a Christmas Cracker the previous Christmas. Not one of the most sophisticated instruments, but all you really needed was a needle that pointed 'North', and the rest was straight forward. Right?

We all met up at the EDS compound. For this trip we had decided to take two spare tyres, just in case, as well as the two spare tyre inner tubes we always carried, as we expected to meet some rough terrain. We also took spare universal couplings. These were part of the transmission, and located on the propeller shaft. From experience we had found that 'sealed for life' components did not last too long in the Saudi Arabian desert, and both Stuart and I could change one of these in 30 minutes. We also each had two five-gallon jerry cans of petrol, although doubted if we would need them for this relatively short trip in the desert. We also carried two five-gallon water containers each.

The only decent road was the coast road which headed north, so I decided to follow it until I thought Al Waba would be directly east of us, and just pick up one of the Bedouin tracks, which would take us there, eventually. After all, it was only about 220 miles, as the crow flies. We drove about 150 miles, up to a petrol station on the main road, where we all filled up with petrol before heading into the desert.

Traffic on the desert track was as busy as we expected. Nothing what-so-ever. The track was barely discernible from the rest of the desert. We headed east for about four hours, covering about 60 miles, before we decided to set up camp for the evening. Evenings in the desert were always a highlight of any trip. The sky was clear, as it seldom rained in the Jeddah area. In fact, it only rained twice during the more than five years I was there. Both times in November!

There was no light pollution and the stars shone magnificently once it became dark, which was always between 6pm and 7pm. We normally sat with our BBQ chicken or burgers, sipping a glass of home brewed wine, pointing out the constellations and planets to each other while chatting.

We set off the next morning, expecting to find Al Waba by about lunch time, but could see nothing. After a couple of hours, I stopped the convoy.

> "Just going to have a look and see where we are", I told everyone, as I climbed onto the roof of my Blazer with my binoculars and compass. "I still can't see anything that looks even remotely like the map", I said to no one in particular, "it's just dead flat, not a volcano in sight!". I took my compass out of my pocket.
>
> "What the Hell is that!", Stuart exclaimed.
>
> "Compass", I replied, "I told you I was bringing one!"
>
> "Looks like something out of a Christmas cracker!", Harvey joked.

I then owned up, that it was in fact a compass out of a Christmas cracker! I think they both expected something a little more sophisticated, that was bigger than a half inch diameter.

We continued heading in an easterly direction, with me stopping every hour or so to have a look around from the roof of the Blazer. I actually had no idea where we were, but did not let anyone else know that. Nothing on the landscape seemed to relate to the map I had in my hand, but each time I checked our location with the map and compass, I confidently confirmed we were on track. Suddenly, directly in front of us, as darkness was starting to fall, there was a black cinder looking wall about eight feet high.

> "We are here, or at least nearby", I announced to everyone. "This must be the lava flow from the volcano, but it's getting too dark to explore now. We'll do that tomorrow".

We set up camp again, and just enjoyed what the desert had to offer before retiring.

Next morning everyone was up fairly early. We had our cooked breakfasts and coffee, then attempted to climb the lava mound. It was too high and rough, so we packed all our gear and drove a few more miles to where the lava wall was not as high. We could not see any volcano, and I was beginning to think that a meteor impact may have been the correct theory, and what we were seeing was the debris of the meteor.

Even when we scaled the black volcanic rock, we could not see anything resembling a volcano, and the rock was too sharp and uneven to walk far on. We continued driving, but stopping every few miles for about three hours looking for the volcano. The compass wasn't very good any way, as we couldn't travel in a straight line. We couldn't see a volcano, but we could see where the lava just stopped a couple of miles ahead. We continued weaving around the maze of lava very slowly, then, as suddenly as the lava wall had started, it stopped. Cautiously, we drove towards the gap in the lava wall. Once through the gap, we were on sand which was strewn with lumps of volcanic rock, but no volcano was in sight!

I got up on the roof of my Blazer once again with my binoculars, and could just make out what seemed to be vegetation in the distance.

"This looks good", I shouted to everyone, "I can definitely see something up ahead".

We all got into our vehicles, and I led us towards the greenery. After about half a mile I had to stop suddenly, as the ground had disappeared, and there was a large hole right in front of me.

We had found Al Waba!

None of us thought that the top of a volcano could be at ground level, but it was. There was just a gentle, almost imperceptible, incline to the rim of the volcano, which was over a mile across and about three hundred yards deep. There was vegetation growing on the inner steep sides of the crater, which looked like it had salt crystals in the centre, shining with a white opalescent glow in the sunlight.

Absolutely beautiful!

As it was mid-afternoon, we just decided to set up camp for the evening before exploring around the rim.

In some areas the sides were not as steep, so we elected to climb down to the volcano floor the following morning, in case darkness fell before we could make it back to camp. Most of us spent a couple of hours walking around the rim, while Antony and Andria took turns riding Antony's motorcycle across the rock-strewn sand near where we had stopped. We were quite surprised to find so much greenery around the rim, considering we had seen so little since we had left the main road. There were palm trees and numerous shrubs growing up the side of the volcano.

The next morning most of us decided to venture down into the crater. It proved to be a lot slower and trickier than we had a first thought, but we did take plenty of water and snacks with us. We expected it to take about two or three hours, but it ended up taking about five. It was well worth the effort, and walking on the opalescent salty sand on the base was an experience worth having.

We had our usual BBQ on our return and spent the rest of the day just relaxing or wandering about the volcanic rocks.

As we had to be home by the next day, we decided to set off early the following morning. Although we had got a little 'temporarily displaced' (I would never say 'lost') on the way to Al Waba, the way back was a lot more straightforward. It seemed a far lot easier navigating the lava outcrops going back than coming. This was probably because I just headed west, in the general direction of where I knew the road to be. It was a lot easier finding a 150 mile long road than it was finding a one mile diameter hole in the middle of the desert!

After driving across the sand for about five hours we hit the main road, about twenty miles nearer to Jeddah than where we had left it. It was an easy two hours' drive from there to home. All the time we were in the desert we did not encounter anyone else.

A couple of years later I repeated this trip, and that time it took only one day to reach Al Waba, and I didn't get 'temporarily displaced'. I even used the same compass, which I still have!

Back at work, things were progressing quite well. I was only the Operations Manager for about six months until EDS employed someone to fill the roll. It was actually another Brit. He was called Mike, and was a lot more 'political' than I ever was. He knew the right things to say to the right people. This meant I could concentrate on what I was brought to the airport for, setting up the data communications network. However, the Saudi Senior Managers did not want too many foreign managerial staff reporting to them, so I was asked to report to Mike, rather than directly to Prince Waleed. Definitely not a problem as far as I was concerned.

In early 1982 a box appeared on my office desk labelled 'IBM Personal Computer'. I had no idea who or what it was for, or what I was supposed to do with it. I assumed it was for Price Waleed, and I would be expected to install it on his desk. Later in the day Mike wandered into my office.

"I see the IBM Personal Computer has arrived". He couldn't miss it sitting in the middle of my desk.

"What is it?", I asked, "And what is it for?".

"IBM just announced these a few months ago, and the Board of Directors have bought a couple, just to try them out", Mike told me.

"Who is it for then?", I enquired, "Prince Alwaleed?".

"No", Mike responded, "It's for you! You will be producing the monthly Computer Terminal Usage Reports and statistics on it. Saudi Senior Management want to know what's happening on all these computer terminals you are installing!"

"All of the Saudi Senior Managers now have terminals, and that information is already available to them through their terminals." I said.

"They want graphs and pie charts and that sort of thing", continued Mike, "So you now have a new toy. It's the first one in Saudi Arabia, and an IBM Systems Engineer will come and install it and show you how it works." said Mike, and left.

The next day the IBM guy arrived, and together we took the IBM PC, which is how he referred to it, out of the box. Together, we installed it, as he had no more idea of how it worked than I did, and the day was spent trying to figure out how the MS-DOS Operating System worked.

It proved to be a great new toy for me, and almost everyone in the Computer Centre came in to have a look at it over the next week. The colour screen fascinated all, as the computer terminals were green text on a grey background. A few weeks later I was presented with a colour printer to print all my Senior Management reports on! I produced all sorts of graphs and colourful charts for the Saudi Board of Directors on this miracle of modern technology. The terminal Usage Reports did, however, not go down too well. This was because almost all of the computer terminals in the Senior Managers offices were seldom, if ever, used!

One day whilst I was in my office, (this wasn't very often, as I was normally driving around the airport site arranging for Contractors to have terminals installed), I was visited by an Irish guy called Mick, (yes, really).

I had met Mick on my travels around the airport site, and socially. I liked Mick. He was about forty years old, average build, long curly dark brown hair, and a permanent stubble, which was never quite a beard. Mick was easy to talk to and always had a story to tell. He liked a drink and laughed a lot. Mick worked for the company which was going to supply 'Mobile Lounges' to the airport. These Mobile Lounges would be at the airport boarding gates, and instead of using buses to transport passengers to the plane, the Mobile Lounge would be driven to the plane and attached to the aircraft door to enable direct embarkation.

Mick didn't come to see me about this, though!

"Hi Mick, haven't seen you for a while." I greeted him.

"Hi Jeff," responded Mick, "I've just been to Administration to sort out some bits and pieces, and thought I would drop in to see you."

I was immediately suspicious! Mick had never just 'dropped in' before. He was obviously after something.

"Remember last week," he reminisced, "We were talking about flying, and you said you were thinking of taking flying lessons in the States if you could afford to take the six-week intensive course?".

We had been talking about this, as a friend of mine had recently learned to fly, getting his Private Pilot's license after taking an intensive course. I quite fancied learning to fly, but as it was pointed out to me, it is an expensive hobby!

"True," I responded, "I would love to learn to fly, but I think it was only wishful thinking, as I couldn't justify the expense."

"A friend of mine can help you out there." Mick continued, "He wants a pilot to do some flying for him, but only someone he can trust, and I recommended you!"

"It pays a lot more than you are earning here!", expanded Mick. "The job is just making deliveries from the USA to Africa, for two days a week. It's a twelve-month contract."

"Why doesn't he hire someone who can fly a plane?" I queried. "I would have to break my contract here, probably work a months' notice, then spend six weeks learning to fly a small single engine aircraft before I could even start working for him."

"There is no-one he trusts enough for this job, who can fly a plane, which is why he asked me to help him out." replied Mick.

We continued discussing the ins and outs of the job. Mick's friend was willing to advance me my first four weeks salary, so I could afford to pay for the lessons, so he was obviously genuine in this job offer.

After discussing this for about half an hour, I eventually got to the bottom on this strange job offer. Mick's nameless friend wanted someone without any sort of criminal record, who Mick could vouch for, to deliver weapons from the USA to one of the African countries.

"Why don't you do it Mick?", I asked.

"I would have," he replied, "but I do have a criminal record from when I mixed with the wrong people when I was in my early twenties."

The plane to be used was an old Douglas DC3 cargo plane, and I was to be paid £3,000 a week, with a generous monthly bonus.

I believe I was being recruited as a gun runner!

I declined, and made it my business to avoid meeting Mick wherever possible.

On one of our regular desert trips, Stuart, Jenny, Judi, and I were joined by another couple who I had met at work.

Jack was Canadian and his wife Kate was English, and both were in their early 30's. Jack was of athletic build, clean shaven with light brown hair and brown eyes. Kate was medium height, quite slender, and attractive, with blonde hair and blue eyes. They were quite new to Saudi Arabia, but they had bought an American GMC four-wheel drive vehicle so they could explore. This was their first inland desert trip. We had decided to visit Wadi Turabah, which was about 200 miles away. It was about a hundred miles east to Taif, then another hundred miles about south-east from Taif.

A wadi is normally a dried up river, which only has water in it in the rainy season, although Wadi Turabah was a 'wet' wadi. It was always wet, being fed by the water flow from the mountain, Jabal Ibrahim. We went to Wadi Turabah several times and never saw a full flow of water, but there was always a great abundance of wildlife and Bedouin.

It was a very pleasant trip which was made even more memorable because of an encounter we had with a Bedouin tribe. It was not unusual for us to meet Bedouin on our travels, and between Stuart and myself, we could normally converse in Arabic in a basic manner.

We were stopped in the middle of nowhere, when this Bedouin man just appeared. He greeted us cordially and asked us to join him in his tent for coffee. He beckoned us to follow him in our vehicles. He had a Toyota Hi-Lux parked just out of sight, and we drove for about ten minutes, following him to where his tribe were camped.

There were only about six tents, and he showed us to our allocated cushions around a low table. He was fascinated with Kate. Blondes were not common in Saudi Arabia! We were served cardamom coffee, which was filtered through the hairs from a camel's tail, and offered dates, which had a liberal covering of flies! Nothing unusual here we thought, just like the many other Bedouin encounters we had experienced.

The Bedouin man wanted to know who Kate was married to. We

told him it was Jack, who we pointed out to him. The Arab then started talking intently to Jack, who didn't have a clue what he was talking about. Stuart and I both thought we had not understood what was being said, but we had. Jack was being asked how much he wanted for his wife! He was initially offered two goats and a camel, then two camels, and finally a camel and a Toyota Hi-Lux! The Bedouin was quite surprised that his offer was refused, but took it in good grace, after all, you cannot come out best in every negotiation!

This was a talking point for years after this trip was just a distant memory.

Wadi Turabah is now a Nature Reserve.

Antony and I often dived when he came to visit us between terms at school. A few weeks earlier I had been on a night dive, and thought it was a great experience, so I suggested it to Antony.

> "How about a night dive, Ant?"
>
> "Sounds good." he responded. "Do we have underwater torches?"
>
> "Yes, I have one, and I can borrow another from my normal dive buddy." I responded.

I rummaged out my underwater torch, which was not an expensive one, and borrowed the other, which was an expensive 'top of the range' one.

It was a bright moonlit night when we decided to go down to a diving place I frequented just outside of town, where the reef was not too far out from the shoreline. We didn't need the torches at all to see our way through the shallows to the edge of the reef. We launched ourselves off and headed downwards to a depth of about fifty feet, where most of the night life seemed to be. It was quite amazing. Completely different from a day dive, as the fish and sea creatures all seemed to have their own bioluminescence, making them look scary, although I recognised most as harmless sea dwellers.

We kept close together, as we should, especially on a night dive. Suddenly, my torch flickered, and a few moments later, it was dead. Bloody cheap torch I said to myself! Should have spent more and got an expensive one like my dive buddy. Never mind, we still had the other torch, and there was a lot to see. We continued with the dive, but were even closer together now, as even the moonlight from the almost full moon did not penetrate fifty feet down. Ten minutes later Antony's torch flickered and died! This was a new, and unpleasant, situation neither of us had been in before.

What the Hell do we do?

We were at neutral buoyancy, which meant we were neither ascending nor descending, nor could we see our bubbles to check which way was up. I was very conscious that we could start swimming down rather than up, or swim up too quickly.

We resolved the situation by slightly increasing the air in our buoyancy compensators, and keeping a close eye on our depth gauges to check our ascent was not too fast. Once we reached about twenty feet below the surface, we could see the moonlight filtering through the water. Never was moonlight so welcome.

Although I was told that two torches failing on a single dive was one in umpteen thousand, I never did another night dive.

Receiving mail at work was quite a rare event, so I was quite excited when a rather impressive envelope with gold edging and my name written on it in a beautiful copperplate script appeared on my desk. Obviously not delivered through the external mail, as it had no stamp or franking on it. I eagerly, but carefully, opened it. Inside was an invitation from Prince Alwaleed to Judi and myself for dinner the following Thursday (Saturday equivalent) at Prince AlWaleed's brothers' house. Although I had been to a few Saudi friends' houses, they were not related to princes! The brother of Prince Waleed was the sponsor for EDS. The address was on the invitation, which I showed to some of my Saudi colleagues.

> "You've been invited to Prince Alwaleed's brothers' home!", gasped Ibrahim.
>
> "You are privileged!", added Jalal.
>
> "Do you see where he lives?", chirped in Ibrahim, "It's the best part of the city suburbs. It's where all the new houses are being built for the really rich Saudi's."

I did a bit of enquiring around, and discovered that four couples had been invited, that I was aware of. Judi and I, another English couple who worked at the British Embassy, my EDS American manager Ryan and his wife, and another American couple who I did not know.

I spoke to Ryan about the invite and he arranged for an EDS driver to take us to the address on the invitation on the evening of the dinner. Thursday came around, and the EDS driver took us there, arriving shortly before the stated time of 9pm. We were driven to a part of the city we had never been to before. The four of us were astounded by the size of the plots where the houses were, each plot had a ten-foot-high wall around it. Once admitted to the property through the huge metal gates by the gatekeeper, we could see the house, or should I say, palace! It was massive! Vast ornamental grounds with a pebbled drive up to the huge impressive front doors. We were met at the door by the prince's brother and his wife, both in very expensive looking traditional clothing. Prince Waleed and his wife were also there, and made the introductions.

The reception area was also huge, with a large ornate crystal chandelier at its centre. We were ushered into a room where we were given figs, dates, olives, and nuts to nibble on, and offered tea. We accepted our tea, and chatted for a few minutes before our other guests arrived. Apart from the four couples we expected to see, there was another couple, who were Saudi. All of the Saudis spoke perfect English, with an English accent as opposed to an American one, which was quite unusual.

After an hour or so, we were brought a small bowl of caviar and biscuits, and we continued chatting, and then we were offered a glass of wine! Obviously a non-alcoholic one, we thought, but it was actually a good quality French wine, complete with alcohol. We finished our caviar and a couple of glasses of wine, and were shown to the dining room.

It was now about 11pm, and having not eaten since about 2pm, the wine was taking its effect on us all. The fourteen of us sat at the table, which was glass and could seat at least twenty people. We each had a Wedgwood bone china plate, a knife and spoon, and Waterford crystal glasses, one for water, two for wine, and what looked like a whisky tumbler, but there was no tablecloth or place settings.

As soon as we sat down two waiters appeared with the food. It was a whole goat, which looked like it had been roasted on a spit, and plates full of rice and flatbreads. It was a 'help yourself' affair. You used your knife or hands to hack off lumps of meat, and grabbed several handfuls of rice and some bread. The delicacy of the goat, the eyes, were offered to the western guests, and we all graciously declined, but the Arabic contingent soon devoured them! The waiters came around the table with bottled water and a choice of red or white wine. Although not what we expected, both Judi and I enjoyed our meal. The other English couple also enjoyed it, but the Americans seemed a bit uncomfortable with the whole thing.

We sat at the table for about an hour, eating goat and rice and drinking wine. The glass table was a mess, with bits of rice and greasy meat spread all over it, together with puddles of spilt wine and water.

It was well after midnight when our host asked us to return to the lounge area where we continued chatting and drinking whisky and brandy. I was feeling a little merry by now and said to our host,

> "I thought alcohol was against the Muslim religion, and was illegal."
>
> "The reason the Muslin religion does not allow alcohol," he replied, "Is because alcohol and hot climates do not mix.

> Drinking alcohol in the desert had serious dehydration consequences a thousand years ago, but if alcohol is consumed at home in the present day, I don't see a problem. The law about alcohol is a very old one, and really could do with being changed. Religion, in this case, has been ensuring the health and wellbeing of its followers."

To me, that seemed a very sensible argument for alcohol in the country, but I knew alcohol was VERY illegal, and if I was found with any, I would have to serve a six months prison term, before being deported. It did seem a little hypocritical to me, but not really my concern, and my host did not seem to have any problem acquiring any kind of alcoholic beverage he wanted. He then went on to say,

"Would you like to see my wine cellar?"

I just about fell over! Wine cellar! In Jeddah! This I must see. He asked me to follow him down a hallway, which must have had twelve doors leading off it, up to a door at the end. He unlocked this door, and there were a few steps down into a room about twenty feet by ten, which had the walls lined with wine racks. These were almost full with several hundred bottles of wine and dozens of bottles of various spirits. I was at a loss what to say, and just said,

"You are never going to go thirsty!".

We returned to the lounge for a while, before we were again ushered into the dining room, which was now as spotless as it was on our arrival, but the table now had several large crystal bowls full of various fruits on it. We sat in our places, and were served ice cream to accompany the fruit, followed almost immediately by a selection of cheeses and a glass of port. It was now approaching 2am. After our desert, we were again shown back into the lounge where we were served coffee and liqueurs. We eventually left at about 4am, in a very happy state indeed!

Shortly after the above event, but not associated with it, the

EDS airport project contract finished. A new company, Arabian Data Systems (ADS) had acquired the contract. ADS was a wholly Saudi Arabian owned company which, understandably, was the direction in which the Saudi Government wished to progress. However, ADS did not have enough capable staff for the work involved, and several EDS staff were asked to transfer from EDS to ADS. I was one of those. EDS were very amenable to this, as they had just won another big contract setting up the Government Social Insurance scheme. One condition that EDS were awarded this contract was that they released the EDS staff the airport wanted, to work on the airport project directly, but under control of ADS!

Not a problem at all as far as I was concerned. The contract conditions were the same as I had with EDS, plus a 25% salary increase. However, we did have to leave the EDS compound and live in the 'old' German Hochtief compound on the airport. Judi quite liked this, as these were well detached brick built bungalows, which had their own gardens. We had never had a garden in Saudi Arabia! Living here also gave us use of an Olympic size swimming pool, and squash, tennis, and racquetball courts. Originally, German contractors lived on the Hochtief compound, but only a few Germans still remained there, as by 1983 the majority of the airport construction work was complete. Hochtief were the major contractor for the construction of the airport, and it was one of the largest contracts ever awarded at the time.

Only one slight snag came to light regarding the transfer of EDS staff working directly for the Saudi Arabian Government. They insisted that all foreign senior management staff had been educated to University Degree standard, and wanted to see the actual degree document. I was classed as senior management but I only have seven GCE O-Levels and a City & Guilds Industrial Measurement and Control Technicians Certificate! Well below Degree standard. But I had lived and worked in Saudi Arabia for four years, and had made numerous friends and contacts who could supply almost anything. I knew a very artistic Filipino guy, who specialised in copying documents, all I needed was an original. A friend of mine had a degree from Queen Mary College, University of London, and for a fee of about £30 my Filipino contact copied it, and put my name on it. It was perfect, and passed the scrutiny of the appropriate authorities.

My 'degree' still hangs on my office wall at home to this day.

I awoke one morning, and discovered it was painful when I went to urinate! My foreskin was no longer supple, and this was not good, especially as I was married! I took the morning off work to go and see my doctor, who was British. After a very brief examination he said,

"Your foreskin has an infection! Very common in hot climates, which is one of the reasons Muslims are circumcised. You will need to be circumcised as soon as possible. I'll organise it for you."

"At my age!" I exclaimed. "I'm almost forty years old!"

"It's the only thing that can be done." the doctor continued, "It's not a big operation."

The next morning, I was admitted to hospital, and introduced to the Arab doctor who was going to perform my operation.

"Have you done many of these before?" I enquired.

"Nothing to worry about, Jeff", he assured me, "I've done hundreds. Every guy has one out here, sooner or later!"

The operation was done later that day, and as I was nodding off under the anaesthetic, I remember mumbling to the doctor, "Don't forget, this is a circumcision, not a castration!"

After the operation, and I had recovered from the anaesthetic, I was visited by Judi and Stuart.

"How did it go?" enquired Stuart, "Does it hurt?"

"Yes, it bloody well does!" I responded, "Now the anaesthetic has worn off, and it's swollen!"

"Give me a look, then." he asked, and asked, and asked. In the end I gave him a look.

"Bloody Hell, it's massive Jeff!" he exclaimed, "And it's almost black, are you sure it's still yours?"

"It might not be," I responded, "Haven't you noticed the donkey in the next bed? He was the donor!"

We all had a good laugh at my expense, and when I was discharged the next day, I spent the following week walking around bow legged!

Although Judi, I, and sometimes Antony went on numerous 'adventures' into the desert, one of the most memorable for me was what we called the "Lawrence" trip. We, the Saudi Arabian Natural History Society, decided to do a trip which was to follow part of the route of the old Ottoman Empire Hejaz Railway.

The Hejaz railway was built in the early 1900's with the objective of creating a railway link between Damascus in Syria, and Medina in Saudi Arabia. I don't believe it was ever fully completed, but it was used strategically by the Turkish during World War I. Lawrence of Arabia led an army of Arabs whose only intent during WW I was to destroy this railway. We were told some bits of locomotive and carriages were still in the desert, but I doubted this!

We decided to follow the route of the railway north from Medina to Medain Saleh. There were only the two vehicles, Stuart, Jenny, and Andria in one; Judi, Antony, and I in the other. Stuart had managed to find a location just outside of Medina which we would use as our starting point, although it was about a five-hour drive to Medina from Jeddah.

As usual we choose a long weekend for our trip, and an early start. We drove almost non-stop to the place we were told to turn off into the desert, which was a petrol station and a local cafe.

"Let's have a meal in the cafe before we head into the desert",

Stuart suggested. It was mid-afternoon, and we hadn't eaten since early morning, so we all agreed.

"I don't suppose there will be much selection on the menu," I said, "Probably chicken, goat, or eggs!"

I was right. We decided we didn't want eggs, the chicken was always like leather, so we opted for goat and rice. We had tea while we waited for our food, and we were offered a hookah pipe, which we refused. As a non-smoker, it was something I had tried once, but didn't like! After about half an hour our food arrived.

"What's this?", Judi and Jenny said almost together.

"It's goat!", responded Stuart.

"But it's a whole half goat which has been spit roasted", exclaimed Judi. "I was expecting some pieces of meat on a plate with rice!"

The rice arrived on a huge plate as Judi was speaking. None of us wanted the eye! There was only one as we had only ordered a half goat. We just tore the meat from the bones, and Stuart found the penis. Stuart tried eating it, but it was chewy and looked like corrugated cardboard. I declined, as did everyone else.

After filling up with fuel we headed into the desert, and after about an hour we found what obviously used to be a railway line. It was a mound of rock and gravel, and traces of where railway sleepers must have been. We started following this mound into the desert and shortly came across a couple of pieces of twisted metal railway line, lying near to the mound. We assumed that the sleepers had been taken for fuel or building purposes, as there were none in sight.

It was getting late so we set up camp, near to a clump of rough vegetation. During our evening meal we were surprised by a rustling noise near our camp fire. Judi looked down to see a spider just walking over her foot! It was a BIG spider, about six inches long including the legs, and the body was about three inches long. Judi screamed, and we all ran away. It was a Camel Spider. The only one we had ever seen during our four years camping in the desert. They are carnivorous, do have a nasty bite, and eat their prey by ingesting it, but they do not eat live camels! That is a myth. However, they move pretty fast, and are scary.

The next morning, we continued following the route of the railway. In most places it was obvious because of the mound of stones and gravel, and we came across the odd piece of track, and the occasional railway sleeper jutting out of the mound of gravel. The sleepers appeared to be a mix of wooden ones and concrete ones, but only a few of the concrete ones remained, and almost no trace at all of the wooden ones. We came across the occasional sleeper spike just lying in the sand. It was late afternoon when Stuart noticed something up ahead.

"Looks like a broken-down vehicle ahead," he shouted to us, "There may be someone in trouble."

I got my binoculars out.

"It looks like a large rusted box to me. It's not a broken-down vehicle! Maybe an old water tower?" I suggested. "We'll see when we get closer."

We got closer and saw that the rusting box was in fact an engine tender, just lying on its side in the sand, and a little way beyond was a locomotive, also lying on its side, quietly rusting away. It was 1983 and we thought that this engine was probably one which had been blown up by Lawrence of Arabia's Arab forces during the Arab Revolt of 1916-18. It had probably been there for the last 65 years, or at least that is what we chose to think, and still do!

We camped beside the locomotive for the night before continuing our adventure the next morning. We continued following the remnants of the railway track north, and eventually came across a building near the track. The building looked fairly intact, with just part of the roof missing. It was open at the front where the large doors had been, and inside we discovered an intact locomotive! It was 'parked' on a short run of railway track, and it had obviously not been moved for many years. It was rusting, but looked complete. We were both astounded and overjoyed that we had found it. This discovery had far exceeded our expectations for the trip.

We stayed only a couple of hours, just to explore and take photographs, before turning round and heading back south, as we were running out of time. The trip home was uneventful, but we definitely thought it was a worthwhile expedition. I wouldn't be surprised if what we found is still there, almost forty years after.

Judi and I enjoyed our time in Saudi Arabia. Judi because she enjoyed the social life, which consisted of never-ending dinner parties, pool parties, and numerous holidays in Europe and beyond. During our time in Saudi, we had holidays in Greece, Italy, Malta, Cyprus, Singapore, Hong Kong, Malaysia, and the USA. Judi was also a sun worshiper, and there was plenty of that in Saudi, either lying by a swimming pool, or lounging on a Red Sea beach.

I enjoyed Saudi because of the desert adventures we had, scuba diving and snorkelling, windsurfing, and motorcycling across the sand dunes. I also love cars, and we always had two vehicles, a weekend four-wheel drive, and a sports car. We always had Chevrolets (apart from the first few weeks), and over the five years we were there we had two Blazers, two Camaros, and a Corvette Stingray.

One month before I had been working at the airport for five years, I was told my contract would be terminated, as this was the maximum time foreign staff were permitted to hold senior positions. I left on good terms and I was given a full repatriation package.

I did look for other work abroad, but Judi was quite keen to return to the UK, so I did not pursue the job I applied for with the Hong Kong Jockey Club, although I have often wondered how that might have turned out.

We left Saudi Arabia in August 1984.

Chapter Five

Back Home

It was the end of August 1984 when Judi and I returned to England. No problems with exit visas from Saudi Arabia. A Lot different than when we left Iran!

Although we owned a house in England, it was rented out, and was probably in the wrong place. Five years earlier we had sold our house, which was near IBM in Sale, Manchester, and bought another one on the outskirts of Coventry. This was because IBM had centralised its operation and moved to Warwick, which was about ten miles away, and IBM said I could have my old job back, if I wanted it. I thought it would be a little boring after what I had been doing abroad, so I did not pursue this very generous offer. Judi and I decided to sell the Coventry house when I had decided on a job. We also decided that we did not want to return to the north-east, as we both thought the climate would be too cold!

A friend I knew from Jeddah, Doug, said the company he was working for was recruiting and they may be interested in me. The company was Racal Milgo, and their office was in Milton Keynes, and since we needed somewhere to live, we rented a house on a monthly contract in Bletchley, near Milton Keynes to use as a base. It was good meeting Doug and his wife Judy again, as they left Jeddah three years before we did.

I also needed a car, and as I was now used to driving large automatics, I bought a seven year old Daimler until I decided on what I really wanted. It was fern green, very comfortable, easy to drive, but was very uneconomical, returning only about twenty miles to the gallon. Petrol in the UK in 1984 was about 40p a litre, a bit different to Saudi Arabia where it was 3p a litre! However, I loved it.

Using Bletchley as our base, I started job hunting. As I was now 39 years old, I was expecting to find it very difficult, and was pleasantly surprised that my skills were in demand, but not at the salary I was on when I left Jeddah. I had discarded the IBM job, and the Racal Milgo one was not for me, being very similar to the IBM one. I looked at five other positions around the country, two in London, one in Edinburgh, one in Bristol, and one in Crawley. The one that really appealed to me was the Crawley based one, which was for the newly established TSB Trustcard.

I attended the interview for Trustcard in late September, shortly after my 39th birthday. It was with the Personnel Department, who were based in Brighton.

> "Welcome, Mr. Covelle", Joyce from Personnel greeted me. "This is Peter, he will be your Manager, and wanted to attend this initial interview."

After I had given details of my experience, Peter told me what I was being recruited for.

> "TSB have recently issued a credit card, it's called Trustcard. However, we do not have the data communications network in place to process transactions, so we pay Visa to do this for us. It's very expensive, so we are going to set-up a Trustcard communications network to interface with Visa, and then expand it to communicate with the TSB Banking mainframe."

Peter also told me who the supplier of the hardware and software were. I hadn't a clue what he was talking about, but it definitely sounded an interesting challenge!

Peter also went on to say, much to Joyce's discomfort, that they had found no-one suitable during the three months they had been recruiting. I decided to be very honest with Peter and Joyce.

> "I have had no experience with the equipment you are proposing to use", I confessed. "I wouldn't even know what a

'Statistical Multiplexor' is or what it does, but I do have a good IBM communications background, and I learn pretty fast. I am also experienced at managing technical staff, who I'm sure you know, can be difficult at times."

I think it was the experience of managing technical staff which impressed Peter, as he obviously had problems in this area before.

Although the job was the newly created one of 'Communications Manager', I would have only one person reporting to me, until I recruited my own team. So very much a hands-on position to start with.

I would be based in Crawley, but would be in Brighton for a day or two a week. The communications network was to connect staff located in three office sites in Brighton to the IBM mainframe in Crawley, so I would be expected to travel between these locations as required.

We then came to the salary discussion.

"This is a new position," Joyce advised, "and as there are no grades, it will be the same grade as a Bank Manager."

This sounds good, I thought, but of course I had been used to negotiating my salary overseas based on what my employer thought I was worth, and my negotiating skills.

"We will start you near the bottom of the grade, with a review after three months. We are thinking of £13,000, increasing to £15,000 in three months. How does that sound?"

"Sorry, it doesn't sound too good to me at all." I replied, "Although I was not expecting anywhere near my leaving salary in Jeddah, I did expect to get about half of it!"

"What was your last salary?" Joyce enquired.

"£36,000", I answered. Joyce spluttered.

"I would like half of that, without probationary period, and you can fire me in three months if you aren't happy with my performance."

The interview ended, with Joyce saying she would be in contact should they decide to invite me for a second interview.

I received a letter the following week offering me the position, without a second interview, on a starting salary of £17,000, with an annual review. I accepted the job.

The job offer was very detailed, and also included a generous relocation package, as my home address was Coventry, even though I was living in Bletchley. TSB Trustcard also agreed to pay the rent on a house for three months, until I had a chance to buy one. Within two weeks we had moved into a rented house in Lindfield, about twelve miles from Crawley, and twenty miles from Brighton.

My start date was Friday 12th October, and I was to report to Personnel in Brighton at 10am, before starting work in Crawley on the following Monday. Trustcard Personnel were located in an office block behind the Grand Hotel on the Brighton seafront.

I couldn't have picked a more auspicious day to start work if I had tried.

The traffic around Brighton seemed very heavy on that Friday morning, but perhaps that was normal for a Friday morning, I thought. I followed the main road into Brighton down to the seafront and was immediately accosted by a policeman carrying an automatic weapon, which he thrust into my face.

"What's your business here?" he commanded.

"I'm starting a new job today, and the office is just beside the road block behind you." I replied.

"Do you have any identification, Sir", he continued, "There has been an incident here."

I had my driver's licence with me, which I produced for him. He scrutinised it thoroughly before handing it back to me.

"I can escort you to your destination, but your car will have to stay here", he informed me. "Please get out of the car."

I got out of my car and was told to put my hands on the roof, and was searched very thoroughly. At the same time, another armed policeman arrived on the scene with a long metal rod with a mirror mounted on it, which he used to examine the underside of my car. It was then that I noticed the pile of rubble in the street, and a hole upstairs at the front of the Grand Hotel.

I hadn't seen the News that morning, but at about 3am the IRA had detonated a bomb in the hotel where Prime Minister Margaret Thatcher was staying for the Conservative Party Conference. Although the Prime Minister was not injured, five people died in the blast.

The armed policeman escorted me to the Trustcard offices, where I was duly processed by Personnel.

I'm never going to forget my first day with TSB Trustcard!

Judi, Antony, and I lived in the rented Lindfield house until we sold our Coventry house, and bought another in Haywards Heath, only a few miles from our rented house. This only took about three months, and we were in our new Haywards Heath house by January 1985.

Antony was eighteen, and decided he had enough of education, and went to work. Initially working in a restaurant, and then getting an office job with Trustcard in Brighton. After a year or so, unknown to me, he applied for a job as a computer operator with Trustcard, which he got, so I often saw him at work in Crawley.

My first employee was Steve, who worked for TSB Bank, and was a computer operator on the TSB Banks computer in Crawley, which was also located in the same building as the Trustcard computer. Steve had worked for TSB since he left school, and was a very experienced computer operator, but the TSB Bank computer was to be decommissioned and all the Banks applications were to be transferred to the main site in Manchester. Steve didn't want to go to Manchester. Almost immediately after Steve joined me, I interviewed Cliff.

I wanted to employ Cliff but Personnel were not happy about it.

> "Cliff doesn't have any qualifications in computing", Joyce stated, "and his experience is not relevant to a commercial business. He's not the right person for the job."

"Yes, I know he doesn't have any qualifications," I said, "but, then neither do I! Also, his communications experience was gained in the Navy, and he has also spent some time as a computer operator."

"Sorry," replied Joyce, "I'm not going to employ him!"

I thought Cliff was a good choice, and although he lacked experience, he was very keen to learn. I took this matter up with Peter, my boss, reminding him that I was told I could recruit my own team. The problem was resolved to my satisfaction, and Cliff joined the team a few weeks later.

I interviewed and appointed all of the people in my team from this time onwards. There was eventually eight of us installing and supporting the Trustcard network, which ended up with about 600 computer terminals in six locations in Brighton. It was interesting work, and I never got bored.

Judi, Antony, and myself were settled in our new house in Haywards Heath, for a year or so. Judi got bored and took a part-time secretarial job in Haywards Heath; Antony was working as a computer operator for TSB, but had decided that the UK was not the place for him, and in 1986 left to go backpacking around the World, and I started a new hobby, restoring old cars, and bought a 1949 Ford Pilot. I had also sold my old Daimler and had bought an almost new Jaguar XJ6.

1985 was my 40th birthday, and Judi said she had cooked a special meal for just the two of us. At about 7pm my pager sounded.

"Bugger!", I shouted, "Not tonight!" I was on call, for any network emergencies, which were infrequent. I called the control centre.

"What's up?"

"Trustcard House multiplexor is down, and the automatic re-routing isn't working", the Control Centre told me, "You will have to go and fix it." I hung up the phone.

"Sorry Judi, I've got to go and sort this out. I'll be back in an hour, in time for my special dinner",

and left the house in a hurry. It was about a twenty-minute drive to Brighton at this time in the evening, and I was sure a new circuit card in the multiplexor would fix the problem, so I wouldn't be there long.

When I arrived at Trustcard House everything seemed fine with the network up and running. No problems or error messages, but I decided I'd better spend half an hour running diagnostics. Still no problems, so I returned home.

I parked my car in front of the garage and walking in the house.

"Surprise, surprise!" was screamed at me by forty voices!

It was a surprise party, and the emergency was just a hoax to get me out of the house for an hour while everyone else arrived, decorations were hung, and a vast array of food and drink conjured up.

It was a very good evening, and someone had even organised a stripper-gram for me, much to my delight and embarrassment!

After working at Trustcard in Crawley for about a year, I was asked to move my office to Brighton, and since the commute from Haywards Heath was longer, I was offered a house move package. I accepted this, and we moved to a three-bedroom bungalow in Henfield in 1987.

Work was uneventful, but Judi and I did have a good social life, and holidayed all over Europe, and also visited some of the American friends we had made in Jeddah. One couple lived in Texas, another in Oregon, and the third in Ohio.

We had also bought a timeshare apartment in Florida in 1984, which we visited alternate years, until we sold it in 2004.

Antony returned from his backpacking trip, which he spent most of in Australia, in 1987. He had decided he was going to move to Sydney after he had saved some money to do so. He stayed with us until after his 21st birthday, then he went to Australia to work and live. He did return to visit us with Wendy, his girlfriend, in 1989, although this was not the lady he eventually married.

We extended our bungalow in Henfield, putting an upstairs on it, which gave us another three bedrooms and an additional two bathrooms, as well as an additional garage. This was very good for us, as we could easily accommodate four of our American friends when they visited us, and I could indulge my hobby restoring old cars!

By this time, 1989, I had sold my 1949 Ford Pilot and had bought a 1969 Mercedes 280SL sports car, which needed very little work doing to it. Shortly afterwards I found a 1966 Daimler 250 V8 saloon in a scrap yard. It was in very bad condition, but it was only £300, so I bought it so I could carry out a full restoration, which took me about a year. My other interests were Squash and Clay Pigeon Shooting. I played squash during the week, and went to a Clay Shoot about every other Sunday.

One day I was asked to see Peter, the Personnel Manager.

> "Hi Jeff," Peter greeted me, "have you heard about the outsourcing of Trustcards IT services?"
>
> "Yes, Peter." I responded, "Is it going to affect my department much?" I enquired naively. Peter put on his serious face.
>
> "All staff involved in Trustcards Information Technology are to be made redundant, or will be offered jobs with Computacenter, the new computer outsourcing company. This includes all of your department, you, and your manager. You need to make your staff aware of the options available to them. This will happen within the next two months."

Peter then went on to tell me that the Board of Directors had decided to concentrate on its 'core business', which is financial services, and not computing.

I spent the next two months sorting out redundancy packages and liaising with the new outsourcing company to see what the best deals for my staff would be. Everyone either transferred to Computacenter, or took redundancy. However, I was not offered redundancy, nor a transfer, but was offered a job as a Project Manager for TSB Bank, which I accepted.

After two months, all IT was handled by the new company, without any Trustcard technical staff. I worked on TSB projects based in Manchester, Birmingham, and London, although I was still based in the Trustcard offices in Brighton. I found the job very interesting, but it did involve a lot of travel.

I was getting towards the end of the Daimler restoration project. It just needed the external chrome work refitting, and some finishing touches doing to the interior woodwork. I had decided to do this over the week-end when I had returned from a Friday business meeting in Birmingham. It was about 6pm when I got home, and Judi was out with friends. I headed straight to our bedroom to get changed into my overalls to spend an hour working on 'Dixie', as I called the Daimler, when I had a sharp pain in my head. I collapsed onto the bed, unconscious, until Judi came home an hour later. Judi helped me get in bed and the doctor was called.

"I hear you fainted earlier today", the Doctor said when he arrived.

"Not a faint", I corrected him, "I had a severe headache, then passed out."

The Doctor examined me.

"Everything seems okay." he said, "Blood pressure is a bit high, but not too bad."

"I still have a terrible headache, and my neck is stiff. It's painful if I move it to the side, or just try to raise it off my pillow." I informed him.

"Looks like you've pulled a muscle in your neck." he told me, "Probably caused by the four hour drive you had just done! Just take it easy for this evening and take some paracetamol."

He left, and I took some paracetamol, and had a lazy evening watching TV with Judi.

However, the headache did not go away over the weekend, and I did not feel able to attend work on the Monday. I contacted my doctor again, who suggested I have a neck massage, which I arranged for later in the week. The headache persevered for a few more days, but I just ignored it, and decided to do a bit of work on Dixie. Just as I started, the pain became unbearable, and Judi helped me into bed, where I passed out. Judi called 999.

Within twenty minutes an ambulance arrived, and I was still unconscious. I started to awaken as the paramedics talked to me. I don't remember much, just one of the paramedics saying to his colleague,

> "This is more than a pulled neck muscle!", and his colleague replying, "Looks like a bleed on the brain to me."

I was put on a stretcher and bundled into the ambulance, where I was taken to the hospital emergency department in Brighton. I don't remember much after that, other than being given a lumbar puncture, and then a trip in another ambulance to the hospital in Haywards Heath.

I went into, or was put into, a coma, and remember nothing until I woke up a week later. I had suffered a subarachnoid haemorrhage. I spent a couple of weeks in hospital before being allowed home for bed rest.

My recovery took about two months, mainly because I could not walk and had to relearn how to. I feel very lucky to have survived this traumatic experience, more for Judi than me, and even more lucky that the after affects were not too serious. My eyes were very sensitive, and I had to wear dark glasses all the time I was awake. This lasted for six months. My hearing was also affected in an unusual way. I found I had trouble hearing people I was in close proximity to, but able to hear conversations taking place at what would normally be outside of hearing range. This lasted for about ten years. I am also dyslexic, although this has improved over the last thirty years.

My eighth close encounter with death!

It was two months before I was fit enough to return to work at TSB Trustcard in early 1991. I continued doing the IT Project Management job I had been doing for the previous year. Two of the major projects I was working on had finished during my absence, and the others were coming to a close. Many of the new projects which were now running involved Trustcard, but the Bank had decided that the project management of its projects should be handled by the outsourcing company's staff rather than TSB staff.

It was in mid-1992 when I had a call to go and see Peter in Personnel.

> "Hi Peter," I greeted him, "I think I know why you asked me over! Something to do with redundancy, perhaps?"
>
> "Yes, Jeff, we are going to have to let you go." he said, "Although we have lots of projects coming up in Brighton, they have to be managed by Computacenter. I worked out your redundancy package, and we want you to leave at the end of the week."

It was a good package, but I would rather of had a regular income, as I still had a quite large mortgage on my Henfield house. I worked out that if I used all my redundancy payment, plus all of the money we had saved in Saudi Arabia, I could pay off the mortgage, but it would only leave us £300 in the bank. We did this, and I started work the next week as a labourer digging out footings for a company which sold conservatories! It was casual 'cash in hand' work, which paid very little. I had looked for a project management job, and had been offered two, but they were based in London, and I was definitely not going to commute to London unless I got really desperate.

Because I was given a redundancy package, I was not entitled to any unemployment benefits, but I still had to attend the Job

Centre, so my National Insurance contributions would be paid by the Government. The first week I attended, the lady at the Job Centre wrote down all my previous work details, searched the vacancies, and found nothing in computing at all. She told me to look at the trade magazines, and record jobs I applied for, which I had been doing already. She told me to come back the following week.

The following week came around and I attended the Job Centre again.

> "Nothing for you on our books," the clerk said, "have you had any luck with your applications?"
>
> "No," I replied, "There's nothing local at all, and I don't want to move house."
>
> "We are going to have to retrain you." The clerk continued, "What about going on a three-month course as a Plumber?"

I wasn't too forthcoming, and was dismissed by the clerk to go into the outer office and check if there were any suitable vacancies listed on their computer terminal. I looked, and there was nothing. I started chatting to the guy sitting beside me.

> "Are they managing to find anything for you?", I enquired.
>
> "Nothing," he answered, "I've been coming here for three months. They are talking about retraining me, but I don't think it's for me.
>
> "Same here." I responded. "Do they want you to retrain as a Plumber?"
>
> "No," he replied in astonishment, "I am a Plumber! They want me to get some training and qualifications in computing."

I just about fell over!

Returning to her office, I suggested to the clerk what she could do with her plumber retraining suggestion!

I never returned to the Job Centre again.

I had been digging holes in the ground for about six weeks, then one evening I received a phone call from Peter, the Trustcard Personnel manager.

> "Sorry to call you at home," he said, "but could you pop into the office tomorrow, as I need to talk to you about your leaving package?".
>
> "Okay." I said," but it will not be until about 5:30pm, as I'm working until 4:30pm."

I was a little concerned. Had they overpaid my redundancy package, I thought. They can't have it back, as I've spent it all!

The next afternoon I went to see Peter at the Trustcard office in Brighton.

> "Hi Jeff," Peter greeted me cheerily, "I just wanted to talk to you about you leaving us. Have you managed to find another job yet?"

I told Peter I had been offered two jobs in London, which I had refused, and mentioned that I was just doing casual work until I found something suitable. (I didn't say that my casual work was digging holes!)

Funny, I thought, no mention of my redundancy payment, which is what I thought Peter wanted to speak to me about.

> "Why did you want to talk to me?" I ventured. "You mentioned something about my leaving package."
>
> "Actually," responded Peter, "that's not really the reason I wanted to speak to you. I was wondering if you would do some contract work for us, but thought you would dismiss it out of hand if I mentioned it on the phone!"
>
> I was a little taken aback! This was totally unexpected. I responded.
>
> "The reason I was made redundant was because TSB wanted Computacenter to manage all of their projects, so why the change of heart?"

Peter went on to explain that Trustcard were not happy with the way Computacenter were running the Trustcard projects, because they had no existing knowledge of the Trustcard network infrastructure, and seemed unable to integrate the new projects into the existing local Trustcard network. TSB had given Trustcard permission to appoint someone to act as an interface between Trustcard and Computacenter for a short period of time, to ensure things went smoothly!

Sounded like the sort of job I was capable of doing, and would like to do.

> "We want to offer you contract work, on a daily rate equivalent to your leaving salary, if you would like the position. It would be for one month initially, but may be extended for up to three months. It should tide you over until you find a more permanent job."
>
> "Yes," I responded, "but as it's contract work, has no banking benefits, and no paid holidays, I would need a daily rate 50% more than my old daily rate!"

He agreed, and I started my short-term contract with Trustcard, which lasted until 1994, almost two years! I think Trustcard did get good value for money from me, as my previous knowledge of designing and setting up the Trustcard network did ensure that additions and modifications went a lot more smoothly than they would otherwise have done.

It was now 1994, Antony was settled in Australia, and Judi and I were living in Henfield, in what started off as a large 1960's two-bedroomed bungalow, but had been extended considerably. We had built on a loft conversion, which was another three bedrooms, a dressing room, and two further bathrooms. We also had a second garage built, to accommodate my two classic cars, a 1969 Mercedes Benz 280SL convertible, and my 1966 Daimler 250 V8 saloon.

Judi and I travelled a lot, and often visited our American friends in the USA, and they also visited us on a regular basis. After my brain haemorrhage in late 1990, we holidayed in New Zealand for a month, and then a "Land of the Midnight Sun" cruise on the Queen Elizabeth II to celebrate our 25th Wedding Anniversary. We also had a holiday in Cornwall in late 1991, and decided that we might retire there, when the time came.

In 1992 we visited Southern Spain, which we liked a lot, and returned almost every year after until 2016. We also visited the USA that year, and every other year in our timeshare in Florida until 2004, and in 1994 we did a six-weeks driving holiday covering most of the southern USA.

In 1993 we had a memorable holiday with our Americans friends Marvin and Jamesetta on the Norfolk Broads, where we rented a boat for a week. Marvin was a retired US Naval Officer, but he did manage to crash our boat three times, which resulted in a loss of our deposit when we returned it at the end of the week!

That same year Judi and I took Marvin and Jamesetta to Cambridge for a few days where we hired a punt for an afternoon on the river Cam.

> "Can you punt?" asked Marvin.
>
> "No problem!" I replied, "Looks easy. Everyone is just pushing their pole in the water, and the punt just slowly goes along. I'll show you how it's done."

I was perhaps a little over confident and wanted to show off.

The first few pushes were fine, then my pole stuck in the riverbed. I tried to hold on, but couldn't. I was dragged off the punt and just flopped into the water. It was only about four feet deep, but I went right under. There was a good crowd, both on the river bank and other punters, who found it very amusing!

I dragged myself onto our punt and with as much dignity as I could muster, continued punting along the river. I was soaked from head to toe. We punted for only a short period before heading back to our hotel where I changed my clothes. I did get a bit of attention from other pedestrians as we walked through the city centre with me squelching along the footpath!

In late 1994 my contract with Trustcard finally came to an end, and I was again unemployed. Judi and I were thinking of having a small bungalow built and retiring to Cornwall. As I had used my redundancy payment from two years previously to pay off our mortgage, we would have enough money when we sold our house in West Sussex to buy a one in Cornwall.

Not to be!

A week after my Trustcard contract ended I received a phone call from Bruce at Computacenter, the Information Technology company who had the outsourcing contract with TSB.

> "I've been told Trustcard have terminated your contract." He pronounced. "Would you consider continuing doing the same roll, but working for us?" he offered, "Trustcard have actually asked me to employ you!"

It seems that Trustcard didn't want to pay me, but did want me to perform an 'interface' roll with Computacenter, so asked them to employ me. I would still be reporting to Trustcard, but being paid by Computacenter. It seems that the Computacenter outsourcing contract was up for renewal, and employing me would smooth things along!

> "Of course, I'm interested." I responded, "What are the contract details?"
>
> "Ongoing contract, will probably be two months, termination by one weeks' notice either side, same daily rate as Trustcard were paying you." was Bruce's response.
>
> "Agreed," I responded, except I want a 30% increase!"

We chatted for a further ten minutes, and agreed a contact we were both comfortable with. I got a 20% increase, and Bruce was happy because it was only for a very short time, and I could start the next day.

The next day I was back at my desk in Brighton, doing the same job I had been doing for the last two years!

Our retirement move to Cornwall would have to be delayed for a few months.

My two-month Computacenter contract had been running for about two years, when Judi and I decided it was time to consider our move to Cornwall. I had accumulated enough money to buy a plot of land in Cornwall, so that's what we did. It was in a rural hamlet near the north coast, about ten miles from Bude.

Our plan was to build our retirement bungalow to our own specification on the plot. We engaged a local architect, and a builder, and drew up a six month build plan, which I would pay for in stages. The only problem was that we didn't have any money, but there were several stages at which the build could be paused.

We wanted to get things started by having plans drawn up and approved, and then starting the ground works. I financed this by selling both of my classic cars!

It was late 1996 when we put our West Sussex house on the market, and it was sold shortly after the foundations of our Cornwall house were completed, and the walls were in the process of construction.

I informed Computacenter about my plans, and said I would work in Brighton until I moved, unless they wished to terminate my contract before. Bruce, who I had never met face-to-face during the two years I had worked for him, was shocked!

> "Why are you moving to Cornwall?" he questioned, "You are surely not planning on retiring when you are only fifty-two years old, are you?"
>
> I explained, "We want to build our retirement home in Cornwall, and now seems like the right time. I may do a bit of contract work after we move." I added.
>
> "I think we still need you for a month, so could you still work in Brighton for a couple of days a week, and do the report writing and documentation from home on the other days, just until we get a replacement for you?"

I agreed, thinking my replacement would be in place before I moved to Cornwall.

We were still in West Sussex for Judi's fiftieth birthday in January, and moved to Cornwall when the house sale was completed in March 1997. Our house build was completed, and we just had to pay the final 30% from the sale of our West Sussex house.

Computacenter had not managed to get a suitable replacement for me, so I stayed in Brighton for two nights a week, and did the remainder of my work from home. I expected this arrangement to last for a week or two, but it actually lasted for another two years!

Chapter Six

Retirement in Cornwall

Well, my planned retirement didn't really start when we moved to Cornwall because I continued with my contract work until just before Easter 1999, when my contract was terminated with two days' notice!

Here we were, in our house, which we called 'Cobwebs', in the small hamlet of Marshgate in Cornwall. Before we purchased our building plot, we had only once been to Cornwall, in 1991, for a holiday.

During the house construction in 1996/97 we had visited the building site about five times, and had visited the local pub, where we met a few locals and became quite friendly with the landlord and landlady. Our first visit to the local pub, The Horseshoe, was the day we decided to buy the plot of land, and we went to the pub for a beer and sandwich.

"Hi!" I said to the guy behind the bar. "Looks pretty busy here, and I see there's lots of food piled up on that big table. Is this a private function? Sorry to intrude if it is, we can go to another pub."

"Welcome," replied the publican, who was called Vic. "It's a reception party!"

Our first visit to the pub was actually Vic and Pats wedding day, and we walked into the pub where they were having their wedding reception!

We introduced ourselves as the new people to the village, who had just bought the plot of land that had been for sale.

"You'll like it here." Vic continued, whilst introducing us to Pat, his new wife. "The locals are all very friendly. I'm from

Bristol and have been here over twenty years. Just help yourself to the food, and your first drink is on us."

Vic was what I expect a pub landlord to look like! He was average height, quite stocky, with a bit more flesh around the middle than he should have had, and was a bit chubby about the face. He had brushed back dark hair, and a smiley, weathered looking face. He was probably in his late forties.

Pat was about the same age, but small and thin, being just about five feet tall. She had medium length brown hair, and not as jovial as her husband.

Luckily, we had rented a cottage in the village for a couple of nights, as we didn't leave the pub until ten hours later, in a very intoxicated state. We had already started making new friends! We visited the pub every time we went to Cornwall to check on progress of the building of our house.

We moved to Marshgate in the Spring of 1997. Although I was still working, we got involved with village life, and often visited the pub. I joined the pub darts team and Judi joined the local Women's Institute. We were soon entertaining our new friends at home, and being entertained at their homes. Judi continued with her jam a chutney making which she had started in Henfield. I constructed a large yellow trolly which was parked by the road at the end of our drive. It was loaded with an assortment of jams and chutneys, which were paid for using the 'honesty box' fixed to it. Over the years Judi's yellow trolly (or reincarnations of it) became a bit of a local landmark. It even ended up on Google Maps!

Judi's produce became so popular that three local shops asked if they could sell it, and holiday makers to Cornwall always returned year after year to restock. One German family even placed an order of sixty jars for each time they returned to Cornwall in their camper van, which was twice a year.

The shops were buying quantities of two hundred and fifty jars a time, and she was selling about two hundred jars a week from the trolly in the summer, and fifty in the winter! Judi enjoyed cookery, so she added cakes to her produce list, supplying two local tea rooms.

That same year we had our regular late summer holiday in Florida, and we visited Antony and his partner, Louise, in Australia for Christmas and New Year 1997/98. We also met Louise's parents during this visit.

Two of our close friends, Nonie who lives in Dorset, and Stuart who lives in France, both had 50th birthdays in 1998.

The eclipse of the sun which happened in 1999, was a total eclipse in Cornwall, and was the first and only total eclipse of the sun I have experienced. I still recall how breath taking it was, and the total silence where we were in the middle of Dartmoor. The birds all started to sing again as the sun emerged from behind the moon, thinking it was sunrise!

It was about Easter 1999, a few days after my Computacenter contract had ended, and we had a few friends at our house for an evening dinner and drinks. During the general conversation, I mentioned that my Computacenter contract had come to an end, and I was now officially retired, (although I was actually only 54 years old). Bill, a retired policeman, was one of the guests.

"So, you will have nothing to do now." He stated. "You will probably get bored pretty soon!" he predicted.

"Not me." I replied, I'm going to buy an old car to restore, and we are planning on having lots of holidays both in the UK and abroad."

Bill continued,

"I don't suppose you could help me out for one day next week, driving a minibus for the day, could you?"

Bill, who lived in the next village, about a mile away, was the local organiser for the Age Concern minibus, which covered the Camelford area. Camelford is about six miles from Marshgate.

"We are short of a driver for a day trip to one of the local Garden Centres, and twelve lunches have already been booked. I don't like to let down the old folks." He pleaded.

"Am I okay to drive a minibus?" I questioned. "I've not driven one before, and I don't have a Public Service Vehicle Driving Licence."

"Not a problem!" stated Bill, "You don't get paid, so a PSV licence is not required for vehicles with up to fourteen seats, which this one has, and I'll take you out for half an hour, just to make sure you get on okay with the minibus."

This was my first introduction to Age Concern, and I continued driving for them for the next ten years!

Bill had just taken over an older vehicle from Age Concern, which he had purchased with voluntary contributions. He was one of the two drivers who had a disagreement with Age Concern over use of the vehicle. It was normally used only once a week, just to collect elderly people and take them out to the local 'Pop-In' centre, where they could have a cup of tea and a chat with other elderly persons. There was an occasional trip to a local garden centre.

Unfortunately, Age Concern only picked up passengers from a few designated stops, and many potential users of the service were unable to use it because they couldn't get to the pick-up points. The bus was seldom half full, and the frequency of the trips was reduced. The bus had spent most of its time parked in Camelford!

Camelford Age Concern 'broke away', and became independent from, but affiliated to, Age Concern UK and offered a door-to-door service. Most of the trips were fully booked.

True to his word, Bill turned up the next day with the Aveco minibus, and I was taken out for a test drive. As I had actually driven large military vehicles when I was in the Territorial Army, a minibus was not a problem for me, and I enjoyed driving it. Within a month I was driving two or three days a week, and enjoying every minute! The elderly passengers enjoyed their days out, and in particular the 'mystery tours' which I organised.

I called them mystery tours because even I didn't know where we were going until the day! The trip normally involved a scenic tour along the north Cornwall minor coastal roads, or across Dartmoor, but always included a lunch stop somewhere. This had not been done before, as all the other trips had a prearranged destination. My mystery trips were always oversubscribed, and soon became a weekly rather than a monthly event.

In 2000, after a memorable New Year in the Horseshoe pub, Antony and Lou visited us for several weeks. They had not seen our new house, nor had they been to Cornwall, so we travelled a lot within the county, visiting all the tourist destinations. Judi and I still managed to spend three weeks in Florida that year, but I had to delay my plans to buy an old car to restore!

Unfortunately, in 2000, I was diagnosed with skin cancer, and needed three minor operations that year to remove cancerous growths from two areas on my back, and one on my arm. This was the beginning of many skin cancer problems, and I was not 'cured' until 2019, after the eleventh cancerous growth was removed from my body. It was on the end of my nose, and the skill of the National Health Service surgeon who removed and rebuilt the end of my nose, had made this operation almost unnoticeable.

In 2000, we also decided to buy a static caravan on the south Cornwall coast. There were two reasons for this. The first being we wanted somewhere not too far away where we could go for short holidays, and the weather in south Cornwall was a lot better than north Cornwall, even though our caravan was only thirty miles from home. The second reason was that we wanted to rent it to holiday makers during the busy school holiday summer season, when we did not want to be on a caravan site. This worked out well, as the rental income we received more than covered the caravan site rental we paid, and left a reasonable amount for us. As neither Judi or I were old enough to receive our government pension, this also supplemented my reduced TSB pension, which I had taken early.

It was in 2001 that we decided to build a small annex on our bungalow, which we planned to offer as holiday accommodation, and would also add value to the property. It took about eight weeks to have built, and two weeks to decorate and build the ornamental garden at the rear. As our bungalow was on a plot almost a half-acre in size, the annex looked in keeping with the house.

We decided to let a local holiday rental agency handle the letting of the property, but we were not happy with the large commission they charged, nor the customers who they sent us. The annex, which we called 'Little Cobwebs', was small, consisting of a lounge/kitchen/dining area, shower room, and a double bedroom. We specified two adults only, and no dogs, as we still had our cat, Fluffy, and a West Highland Terrier, Millie.

The rental agency sent a couple with a child, who had to sleep on the sofa, and another couple with a large German Shepherd dog! I decided the best idea was to advertise it ourselves on this newfangled Internet, so I taught myself how to create our own website, and promote it with the search engines. This was very successful, and by the third year we had a 90% occupancy rate, with lots of repeat business.

One day I had a phone call from someone wanting to rent our caravan.

> "I want to rent your caravan for next week." This voice on the phone said. It was Friday morning, and he wanted to rent for the week commencing Saturday, the next day.
>
> "I've looked at your website, and this is the only week you have free. Is that correct? If so, I definitely want it."
>
> Short notice bookings were not unusual, but this was VERY short notice.
>
> "Okay, that's fine. It's not enough notice for you to send me a cheque, so can you do a bank transfer for the £350, or I can take a credit card payment."

"I don't have the facility to do a bank transfer, and it's too much for my credit card, so I'll bring the cash with me tomorrow. My name is Greg, and I'll meet you at the caravan at 2pm. Just give me the instructions to get there." was his response.

I gave him the instructions, and the next morning I was at the caravan doing the weekly clean. (I cleaned the caravan and Judi cleaned Little Cobwebs during the summer.) He never turned up! I waited until 8pm, constantly calling the mobile number he had left me, but never got a reply. I was furious, especially as someone else had phoned after he did, who also wanted to rent our caravan.

The next day I called him again. No reply. I called every day for the whole week, and never got a reply. I decided after a week, that he obviously knew my number so wasn't answering. I went next door to my neighbour and asked to borrow her phone. I phoned Greg. He answered.

"Hi, Greg here."

"Hi, Jeff here." I replied, "Remember me?"

"Oh, I decided not to bother with the caravan." Was his startled response. "We went somewhere else instead."

"And you couldn't even be bothered to let me know?" I retorted angrily. "You made a verbal contract with me, so you owe me £350! How are you going to pay me?"

"Sorry, I'll send you a cheque in the post tomorrow."

Of course, the cheque never arrived. I contacted him several times until he said,

"I'm not paying! I decided not to rent your holiday caravan, so I don't think I should pay you!"

"If you don't pay me, I'll take you to court!" was my reply. And I did.

The court ruled in my favour, and Greg was ordered to pay me £350, plus £80 costs. He still refused to pay, so I returned to the court three months later, who again ordered him to pay the

£430, plus an additional £80 costs, plus £25 interest. As he still didn't pay in the next two months, I applied to the court to be able to contact his employer, and was given permission to do so. I contacted Greg's employer, who were not aware of his County Court Judgement, and not happy about it, as Greg worked in their Security department. They arranged to pay me one-twelfth of £535, plus interest, monthly over the next twelve months by deducting the money directly from his salary, and transferring it into my bank account.

Unfortunately for Greg, his company forgot to stop paying me after the twelve months, and paid an extra two months in error. Greg phoned me.

> "You have been paid two payments too many. You need to send them back to me." he requested, without even a please!
>
> My reply was,
>
> "Sue me!"

I never heard from Greg again.

The Eden Project botanical gardens opened in Bodelva in Cornwall in March 2001, and because of my involvement with Age Concern I was invited to take a pre-opening tour there with Judi. It was about two weeks before the official opening, so we had to wear high visibility jackets and hard hats, as construction of one of the biodomes was not complete. Although I am not a gardener, the visit was really worthwhile, and very interesting.

After opening I went there several times with the Age Concern bus, and were given concessionary admission rates, and the driver always went free of charge. I probably visited the Eden Project twenty times during my ten years with Age Concern.

It was 2002. Judi and I were kept pretty busy with our Little Cobwebs holiday home, our caravan, Judi's jams, chutneys and cakes, and our support for the Age Concern bus.

Bill was no longer involved with the bus, and I had taken over responsibility for maintenance, and another guy, John, who lived in Marshgate accepted the responsibility of scheduling the trips. We were very busy, and now had seven drivers.

As the bus was getting a little old and unreliable, it was decided it was time to replace it. I took on the almost full-time roll of fund raiser, and within six months we had raised the £32,000 needed to buy a new bus. I took it upon myself to contact over 250 organisations who I thought might contribute to this worthy charity, including the National Lottery, who contributed £5,000! About thirty of the other organisations I contacted contributed a further £16,000 between them, and we were offered £7,000 for the old bus in part exchange. Judi even organised cream tea afternoons in our garden, and many of the users of the minibus service did their own fundraising raffles and events, raising the remaining £4,000.

In 2003, after we had purchased our new minibus and I had a bit more time, I decided I would like to do the car restoration project, which I had planned on doing four years previously.

I bought a 1970 Mercedes 280SL California. Quite a rare model in right-hand-drive. It had a removable hard top, but not a soft top. I guess it doesn't rain in California! It was in pretty rough, but original condition, which was what I liked. It was my project for the next six months.

What with restoring my old Mercedes; driving the Age Concern bus and looking after its maintenance, which took up about two days a week of my time; our Little Cobwebs holiday let; renting out our caravan; and Judi's jam, chutney, and cakes business, Judi and I were pretty fully occupied in our retirement!

We did, however, still had time to holiday in Spain, Scotland, the Cornish south coast, visit the USA, and have our American friends come to stay. I also invited two of my old friends from my days working at IBM for a reunion at our house in Cornwall. It was good to see them, and we still keep in touch.

By 2004 our small holiday accommodation business was thriving. Little Cobwebs was occupied for about forty-eight weeks a year, and our caravan was fully occupied for the eight weeks we offered it.

We decided to buy a newer caravan, as our old one was now eight years old. We kept the old caravan, and we were able to rent it out for about six months of the year, and still rented out our new one for the eight weeks summer period. Two of our acquaintances on the caravan site also decided they wanted to rent out their caravans, but did not know how to go about it, so I added their caravans to my web site, and handled all the bookings for them, for a 10% commission. Everyone was happy!

I also decided to treat myself to a new Mercedes sports car, to celebrate my retirement. Well, that was my excuse!

There was a serious flood in north Cornwall in 2004. It was in the afternoon of Monday 16th August, when a flash flood engulfed the villages of Boscastle and Crackington Haven. It was totally unexpected, and I was driving the Age Concern Bus. One of my passengers lived in Boscastle (which was three miles from my home), and I was returning her home from a day out. Driving down the narrow road to Boscastle was very busy, and as the road is only wide enough for one vehicle, I stopped someone coming towards us.

"What's the problem?" I enquired of the very agitated driver.

"Flood! The whole of Boscastle is under water! You can't get down there."

"But it's not been raining!" I exclaimed.

It had been raining further up the Valency valley, and the River Valency had risen over seven feet, with rain falling at one inch in fifteen minutes at one point. The River Valency runs into to sea at Boscastle which caused the flash flood. I had to turn around, and took my passenger to stay with her sister in Bude.

The next day I tried to drive to Boscastle, but could only get to within half a mile, as the road and car park had been washed away. The damage was devastating with many buildings damaged, roads and bridges washed away. The flood defence system had been totally ineffective. Although the water level at some of the buildings was up to ten feet, no one died in the flood, nor were there any serious injuries to any people. About 150 cars were washed from the car park into the harbour, but only about ninety were recovered, the remainder were washed out to sea. Many of the cars had dogs in them, which, unfortunately, perished. It took about four years to rebuild Boscastle and install the new flood defence systems.

For the next few years, we just bounced along, enjoying holidays abroad, and time with our friends in England. In 2005 Antony and Lou visited us with Lou's parents, Nev and Loretta, for my 60th birthday party.

The following year was our Ruby Wedding Anniversary, which we celebrated with a very large party at home! That year we also visited our friends Stuart and Jenny who live in France, and spent a month in southern Spain afterwards.

It was Judi's 60th birthday in January 2007, which we spent at home, but we decided we would buy a holiday home in south Cornwall to celebrate the occasion! We bought a small two-bedroom bungalow in the countryside near Looe. It was cheap, and in disgusting condition, but we liked a challenge. I started the renovation process in the February, by tearing out most of the insides, including a substantial wall. By the summer we had a beautiful holiday home, which had been totally refurbished.

We spent three or four days there every two weeks or so, and enjoyed the tranquillity of the location. We kept this holiday home until 2010, and sold it because we had decided to leave Cornwall.

When we moved to Cornwall, it was to be our last move. We had our bungalow built to our own specification, and I loved my garage, which was big enough for four cars. However, there were two things we thought were lacking. One was a close community spirit, and the other was the weather! North Cornwall had pleasant summers, but winter was always wet and windy. It snowed only once during our time in Cornwall. In 2010 we decided we were going to move as soon as we found what we wanted.

We had spent a lot of time in the USA, with our American friends, and touring. One thing that attracted us to the USA were the 'Gated Communities' where many retired Americans lived, particularly in Florida and Texas, and the weather was a lot better than Cornwall. The residents of these gated communities were always friendly and welcoming. We decided to investigate the possibility of moving to the USA on a permanent basis for the remainder of our retirement.

After a few weeks of investigation, we decided it was not practical for several reasons. The two major reasons being the medical system, (we would need to pay about $1,000 a month for medical cover), and our UK pensions, which would have been frozen at their current levels, and would be susceptible to currency fluctuations.

We decided that we would look at gated communities, or something similar, in the UK. We stumbled upon Park Home living, and looked at several in Cornwall. Although some Park Homes had a good community spirit, they still had the Cornish wet winters. We decided to look at where we knew, which was the south east of England. We were always happy with the weather when we lived in West Sussex, but we did not like how busy it was. We compromised, and decided that we would look for a Park Home in East Sussex, on the basis that the weather was similar to West Sussex and it was a quieter county.

In the summer of 2010, we looked at eight different Park Home sites, and we both agreed that there was only one where we wanted to live. It had a community centre, shop, post office, swimming pool, bowling green, and a pub. We had even chosen a house which was empty.

We looked at several homes with Steve, the park owner. Although we said we were not in a position to buy yet, Steve insisted in showing us what was currently for sale. The first house he showed us was in great condition.

"This is probably the best home here", he gushed. "Freshly painted and decorated, and even has electric curtain drawing! It's also only two minutes from the swimming pool." He continued.

"It also has neighbours either side, and backs onto another garden!" I responded.

It was not what we wanted. There were two other three-bedroom properties available. The next one was also in great condition, but was on the main road.

"Another lovely property," said Steve. "It's just become available last week, and will be gone in a few weeks' time!"

"Sorry, not what we want. Too close to the road for us." I pointed out.

The last one he showed us was in terrible condition, as it had been unoccupied for about three years, and had not been maintained before that! There had been a water leak in the kitchen, which meant part of the floor needed replacing; the central heating boiler did not work; most of the windows and frames needed replacing; the facia and guttering all needed replacing; the white exterior was green with moss and needed power hosing before repainting; and the rear of the house was just broken patio slabs and mud. BUT, it was exactly where we wanted it to be! Close to a pond at the front, and backing onto the woods. Only one neighbour, who we shared the garage drive with. The main drawback for me was a garage which could only accommodate one car, although there was room for a work bench as well.

"This is the one we like!" I said to Steve.

He was horrified.

"This is falling apart! No one wants to buy it because it's over-

> priced for the condition it's in, and the seller won't drop his price." he stated. "It's a pity you are not able to buy it, because I don't think anyone else is likely to!"

Steve was keen to sell it, as he received a payment of 10% of the sale price!

Unfortunately, dogs were not allowed, and we still had Millie, our ageing West Highland Terrier. She was fourteen years old, and getting a bit dithery, but we wouldn't go anywhere without her. We decided to put our move on hold for a couple of years until Millie was no longer with us.

We went back home and continued with our perfectly acceptable life style in Cornwall, but looked forward to the day we would be able to move. Millie died suddenly in the autumn of 2011 of liver failure. Although we were broken hearted at her passing, it did allow us to continue with our plans to move to East Sussex.

We put our house on the market immediately.

Chapter Seven

Final Move

It had been over a year since we had looked at park homes in East Sussex, but we knew which park home we wanted to live on, so we returned there shortly after Millie had died. We met Steve again, and he showed us the list of properties which were currently on the market. There were eleven properties for sale, of which three were the larger three-bedroomed ones. Two were properties we had not seen previously, but one of the three was the one we liked the previous year, which was now in even worse condition!

"Still not managed to sell the one which is falling apart Steve?" I commented looking through the list.

"Too much work needs doing on it for anyone to take it on now." He responded, "The rear guttering fell off a couple of months ago, and rainwater is running down the side of the house. It won't be long before it gets dampness inside. The seller has reduced the price by £10,000, but still no one is interested."

Judi and I looked at the other two properties, which were in excellent condition, but we still liked the position of the neglected one. We had a good look at the insides again, and decided we would take on the challenge of restoring it to a habitable home.

"We want to buy the rough one on Deer Haven." I said to Steve. His surprise was obvious! He had just sold a property he thought would never sell. I could see him working out his commission in his head!

We chatted to the next-door neighbours, Dot and Buster, who

had lived there for almost three years, but had never had anyone living next door. They had been complaining to Steve about the condition of the vacant property, and were very pleased that we had decided to buy it.

Our house in Cornwall had been on the market for only four weeks before it was sold to the second person to look at it. They wanted it immediately, and instructed their solicitor to expedite the purchase. They did not have a property to sell, and the buying of a Park Home property was as easy as buying a car!

Consequently, we moved to East Sussex on the same day we sold our house in Cornwall, which was on the 18th January 2012, which was also Judi's birthday! We spent the 18th January in a hotel in Hastings, and moved into our Deanland Wood Park house on the 19th. A date which is easy to remember, as Judi's birthday was on the 18th January, and Antony's is on the 20th January!

We had paid a large deposit on our new house in late December 2011, and had permission to do some of the basic work needed before we moved in. The guttering was repaired temporarily, the kitchen floor was repaired, and a new central heating boiler installed. We started the rest of the work in February. This included replacing all of the window frames and double glazing. The lounge, bedrooms, and kitchen had bay windows installed. The house was repainted outside and inside, and all the external facias and guttering were replaced.

We later refurbished the kitchen, including new oven, hob, fridge freezer, dishwasher, washing machine, and clothes drier. New ceiling lighting was installed, and all the switches and power outlets were replaced with steel ones.

Both large bedrooms and both bathrooms were completely renewed, and the small third bedroom was converted into a small office.

In the summer of 2012, we also had all of the outside area upgraded with a new patio area.

We were happy with our new house in East Sussex.

In the February of 2012 it snowed. Although the park looked pretty under several inches of snow, it was cold in the house! The loft insulation was minimal, and most of the windows had ineffective double-glazed units which were 'blown', and the window frames let in a cold draft. However, we did enjoy the snow, as it was a very rare event in Cornwall. I had also bought a new BMW X3 sports utility vehicle. It was four-wheel drive, and I loved putting it through its paces, much to the horror of any passengers I might have on board. Dot and Buster, our next-door neighbours wanted a ride in my new car, so we did a bit of 'off roading'.

> "We seem to be sliding a bit more than I expected!" Exclaimed Buster. (Dot seemed to be enjoying the thrill.)
>
> "I've got to push the roadholding to the limit." I responded, "I need to know how it will react in an emergency situation on the ice, should one occur!"

Judi and Dot just giggled as I slid sideways across a field covered with snow, then slammed the brakes on while doing a tight turn. Buster's face went a ghostly white colour, which matched the colour of his knuckles, gripping the arm rests.

I was satisfied with the performance of my new car!

Our neighbours, Dot and Buster, were very alike. Both were very thin, and about the same height, the only difference being that Dot was a heavy smoker with a constant cough.

We didn't socialise much with Dot and Buster, but they did introduce us to the K2 Indian restaurant, for which Judi and I were eternally grateful. We were both curry addicts! They also introduced us to Brian and Jean, who also live nearby on the park. Brian and Jean are still very good friends, and we socialised with them a lot, and often had dinner parties at each other's house. Both Judi and Jean were very good cooks. Brian and I are very good eaters!

Brian and I became very good mates, and we both went to the

Deanland Park Keep Fit sessions on Mondays and Fridays, and darts on Friday evening, followed by a few beers in the Inn on the Park.

We still do!

Brian and Jean moved to Deanland from the Warrington area in the north-west in 2011. The main reason for their move to the south-east was Jeans two married daughters and their families who lived nearby, one in Brighton, the other in Crowborough.

Although I had no charity work to do, and Judi stopped making her jams, chutneys and cakes on a commercial basis, we both remained pretty active.

I joined in a lot of the social activities on the park, getting involved in the Keep Fit and Darts, as mentioned, and we also used the swimming pool a lot in the summer. I also did photography, and played petanque, and joined the pub darts team. We also had a lot of holidays, and tried to go away for a week most months, and a couple of months a year in either Spain or Florida.

In 2012 we visited our friends Stuart and Jenny in France for a few weeks in the summer. We also went to Bruges for the day on our Wedding Anniversary with Brian and Jean.

For an extended holiday, we rented a penthouse apartment in Southern Spain for October.

We also decided we would try house sitting, while a lot of work was being carried out on our house in the spring. We accepted a one week stay in a beautiful Tudor house in Herefordshire. In exchange for our stay in the house we looked after the owner's dogs and chickens! The house was really beautiful, but was the most unclean and untidy house inside which we had ever seen! Judi wanted to leave as soon as we arrived, but the owners had already left to go on holiday, so we stayed. We did enjoy looking after the fifty or so chickens and walking the dogs in the Herefordshire countryside, but not time spent in the house!

We never did house sitting again!

2013 was quite a busy year for us, and we spent a lot of time on holidays abroad.

We spent four weeks in Florida in January and February, for Judi's birthday; two weeks in France and Belgium with Nonie & Albert in June; three weeks in September in South Africa with Ian and Annie, who were new friends we had made at Deanland; and six weeks in Spain in the Autumn. We also visited Nonie and Albert several times at their home in Dorset.

Unfortunately, I was being still being treated for skin cancer, and needed several minor operations to remove malignant melanomas. Over the space of about sixteen years, I had nine of these melanomas removed, and several basal cell carcinomas also. The last one I had removed was from my nose, in 2016, and I was officially considered 'cured' in 2019.

We rebooked the villa in Florida which we normally stayed in, for a seven-week holiday in January and February 2014, however, my health took a downward turn when I was diagnosed with a heart condition during the first week of the year.

During the prognosis with Dr Silk, I had an Electrocardiogram (ECG). The reading was irregular, to the point that I was given a second one. This one was also irregular, and I was told the machine was not working and I would have to come back later, when they could get hold of another machine. I returned later for my third ECG, on a different machine, and it also produced results which baffled the heart surgeon. I was then taken for an angiogram, which involved injecting a dye into my bloodstream while having a special type of X-Ray taken.

The angiogram showed that one of my heart arteries was totally blocked, but somehow my body had rerouted the blood the wrong way through a minor artery to maintain a blood supply to the heart! This had confused the ECG machine, producing readings which Dr Silk had never encountered before.

After several other tests, my condition was classed as critical, as three of my heart arteries were in poor condition, one being totally blocked, another 98% blocked, and the third 65% blocked! Within a week of my diagnosis, I was to be admitted to hospital to have two of my arteries 'cleaned', and stents inserted into the seriously blocked (98%) one. It was decided to leave the totally blocked one alone as the 'automatic rerouting' for that one was adequate, and should not be tampered with.

I was summoned to the hospital three days after my condition was confirmed as 'life threatening' and requiring urgent attention. I was ushered to a ward, and told to get into bed immediately! Once in bed the cardiac surgeon who had diagnosed me came to see me.

"How are you feeling?" Dr Silk enquired.

"A bit short of breath." Was my response, "but apart from that, not too bad."

"Are you worried about the operation?" Dr Silk continued.

"Not overly," I truthfully replied, "I've been reading up on bypass operations, and the success rate is pretty high, and the fatality rate is pretty low."

"Not in your case!" retorted Dr Silk. "I am going to clean out two major arteries, and insert three stents into one of them. It's a very serious operation, and I have to make you fully aware of the situation. Your arteries are in very poor condition, and the success rate is 50/50 at best and there is a 10% chance you will not survive the operation."

Not exactly the sugar-coated pep talk I was expecting! I did realise that it is now policy that the patient is fully aware of the outcome of any medical procedures, but I somehow didn't expect such a forthright explanation of the possibilities.

"Do you wish me to perform this operation on you?" continued the doctor. "You do, of course, have to give me written permission."

"What happens if I don't have the operation?" I questioned.

"You will have a heart attack and probably die within a week." Was the response I received, "although if you do nothing and just stay in bed, you could last for up to three months."

I gave my permission for the operation, and later that afternoon it took place.

I was all prepped before I was wheeled down to the operating theatre. I still don't know why I was wearing a pair of paper briefs, which were immediately cut off when I was positioned on the operating table.

There were two things that surprised me in the theatre.

Firstly, the number of people there! There were eleven, and I was introduced to them all! Dr Silk was the lead surgeon, and there was another surgeon; two nurses were assisting; there was an anaesthetist and assistant; a three person 'Crash Team', and two observers, who I think were medical students.

Secondly, I would be awake throughout the operation, and Dr Silk even adjusted his TV monitor, on my request, so I could see what was happening. The reason I was awake was to give Dr Silk feedback on how I was feeling during the procedure.

Prior to entering the operating theatre, I was given some medication to relax me, but not to lose consciousness. I also had a cannula attached to my arm when I got inside the theatre, which I assume was to administer drugs to keep me relaxed and pain free for the duration of the operation. As soon as the drug was inserted, I felt warm and relaxed, and didn't really notice Dr Silk cutting open my groin and inserting a device. I could feel something being pushed into my groin, and I could see it on the monitor. It reminded me of the equipment used by plumbers to unblock drains, in a miniature form. Dr Silk was talking to me all the time explaining what he was doing and constantly asking how I was feeling. He was drilling out my artery, and it seemed to be taking forever. It felt uncomfortable, and was feeling drowsy, then, suddenly I felt an immense pain in my chest. It felt like an elephant was sitting on my chest and I was gasping for breath. My head was spinning, lights were flashing in my head, and in the distance, I could hear Dr Silk shouting at me.

"Talk to me Jeff, talk to me! Move your hand if you can hear me! Talk to me Jeff!"

The pain was unbearable and everything went dark. I did not hear Dr Silk shouting at me anymore.

Then, suddenly, I heard Dr Silk again.

I thought I must have passed out.

"Hello, Jeff! Can you hear me? Are you with us?"

I opened my eyes. Five people were leaning over me. The operating table had been moved to the centre of the operating theatre, and there was equipment all around me. There were pipes and tubing lying across my body. I was aching all over, and two additional cannulas were attached to me; one in my other thigh, and one in my other arm. The pain in my chest had gone.

I managed a nod and a grunt.

"You're back with us! That was a close thing! We thought we had lost you!" continued Dr Silk. "You were actually dead for almost two minutes!"

It seems that the artery collapsed because it was so badly diseased, and instead of putting in three 12mm stents, they had to completely stent the whole artery. I now had 80mm of stents in one artery. What Dr Silk told me was called 'A full metal jacket', and I was alive!

Definitely my ninth brush with death!!

Surprisingly, my recovery was very quick. I was moved from the operating theatre to the intensive post-operative area, and told I would probably be in intensive care for the next twenty-four hours.

Within an hour I had recovered enough to realise that I was hungry! Both the nurses sitting by my bed were unsure what to do, and one went to see Dr Silk, who was in his office to ask if it was okay to feed me!

Dr Silk arrived back with the second nurse within five minutes.

> "You shouldn't be feeling this well so soon after the major trauma you have just had, but the readings on your monitors are all normal, and you look pretty good, so you can have a sandwich before we take you back to the ward! Dinner is in about four hours' time."
>
> Ten minutes later I was eating a cheese sandwich and drinking a cup of tea!

I was discharged late the following day.

A happy outcome for both Dr Silk and me. I was alive, and Dr Silk didn't have a failed operation on his record!

Although the operation was a success, I had to attend 'Cardiac Rehab' twice a week for the following six weeks. Each session was about one hour long. Half was physical exercises, the other half was cardiac education, mainly diet and anti-smoking videos.

As we had missed our holiday in Florida, we decided to have lots of short holidays in the UK during the Spring and Summer, before having an extended break in southern Spain in the Autumn.

We visited The New Forest in March, Dorset in April, and in May we did a five-day cruise through the Scottish lochs, starting at Oban in the west and finishing at Inverness in the east. It was only about one hundred miles, but the scenery was magnificent. The boat we travelled on was 'Lord of the Glens', which carried only fifty passengers, but in luxury! We went with our friends Ian and Annie, who also live at Deanland Wood Park. On our way home we stayed in a hotel in Chollerford, near Hexham, which is only 25 miles from where I was born, so I could revisit my birth place.

During the rest of the summer, we visited Alton, Caen Hill, Longleat, and the Norfolk Broads. We also revisited the Mary Rose at Portsmouth, which we had not seen since our last visit in 1984, when the museum originally opened.

We spent October in a rented villa in Duquesa, Manilva, in Spain.

On our return we decided to spend a few days in London to see the fantastic display of 888,246 ceramic poppies at the Tower of London, which were planted by over 17,000 volunteers. It was a poignant ceremony and a never forgotten sight to have had the privilege to witness.

In early December we spent a week in the Cotswolds, which led us nicely into Christmas, which we spent at home with our friends.

It was about this time that our next door neighbours decided to move, and we soon had new neighbours. Our new neighbours, Keith and Elaine, who were a couple of years older than us, were a lot more likable and sociable than our old ones, and we became friends. They later became very good friends to me!

At the beginning or 2015 we rented a villa in Florida for seven weeks, and were joined by Antony and Lou for about three weeks. We had a great time at the theme parks, and exploring the less commercialised parts of the state. In particular, we enjoyed 'Blue Water', which is home to dozens of manatees. We also visited the Everglades National Park.

After our return home, and a short break in Bath, I was summoned for Jury Service at Lewes Crown Court. I was almost seventy years old and definitely did not expect this! The letter told me what day (it was a Monday), and time to report to the court. I was told I would be there for two weeks, and may be a juror on several cases.

I turned up on the appointed day and time in early April, along with about thirty other prospective jurors. We were ushered into a room and shown a brief video outlining the procedures. We were also told it was illegal to discuss any case we would be involved in outside of the jury room.

Jury selection started immediately after the introductory video. Each of us was given a number and told to wait in the lounge area.

After a short while, the Clerk of the Court appeared and called out fourteen numbers, of which I was one. He then told two of the fourteen to remain, and the other twelve to follow him (accompanied by security personnel), to the courtroom. We were shown into the jury box and told to sit, where we were sworn in, and told to always sit in the same place on the bench. There were also two members of the court sworn in, and these were the only two people we would be allowed to speak to outside of the courtroom regarding any aspect of the trial.

I was very apprehensive about the whole thing, which seemed like a TV courtroom drama to me!

Shortly after the swearing in had finished the Judge appeared.

> "Good morning, Juror's." He greeted us convivially. A little less severe than I was expecting!
>
> "Good morning, Your Honour." We replied. (We had been told how to address the Judge.)

The Judge went on to briefly explain court procedures, then the proceedings started.

Initially the prosecution spoke to a couple of the jurors, and one was asked to leave. He was replaced by one of the two remaining from the original fourteen.

The proceedings started immediately. We were told that the defendant was accused of rape, and we should not form any opinions until after the whole case, from both the defence and the prosecution had been presented to us. Should we wish to communicate with the Judge for any reason, we were to write a note and ask one of the court staff who had been sworn in with us to give it to the Judge. We had to raise our hand to attract the Judges attention, but were not allowed to speak.

The case was complex and very involved. Both the accused and the accuser were Polish, and needed the court interpreter for a lot of the time. There had been a lot of 'texting' between the two parties for a couple of weeks before the incident, and we were given this to read during several breaks. There was over a hundred pages.

The couple lived together and were intimate, and the basis for the prosecution was that the accused was told by the accuser that she did not want to be intimate again, shortly after they had been intimate. However, the accused did not think she was being serious, as it was normal in their relationship to be intimate twice in a very short time.

It was a very technical case, as the legal definition of rape depends on 'penetration', and he denied penetration in the second instance, but she asserted that she was penetrated the second time, after she had said 'No!' The case lasted six days and on the afternoon of the sixth day we were asked to retire and give a verdict, which, the Judge specified, was to be unanimous.

We retired to the jury room where we were told to appoint a spokesperson for the jury, and then started to discuss the case. It was not a straightforward verdict. A six/six split! We all had a slightly different interpretation of the facts, and called for lots of the evidence so we could review it again.

We did not reach a verdict that day, nor the next. We had a 'not guilty' verdict of eight/four at lunchtime on the eighth day, which was not acceptable to the Judge. Deliberations continued through the ninth day, and by late afternoon we had reached a verdict of 'not guilty' by a ten/two majority. The judge accepted this verdict, and the prisoner was released immediately.

After the verdict had been given, we were told the history of the lady who had claimed she had been raped. What surprised us all, was that this was the third time she had brought a rape charge, against three different men who she had being living with over the previous two years. What also surprised me was that the six women in the jury all gave a 'not guilty' verdict, and it was two of the men who stuck by their 'guilty' verdict!

As the one case had taken nine of the ten days of our jury service requirement, and the case was quite intense, we were excused duty for the last day.

A few weeks after my duty as a juror had finished, I was asked to attend Eastbourne District General Hospital (EDGH), as the results of a recent blood test were 'irregular'! After further investigation and X-rays of my back and hips, which I thought were for arthritis, and specialised blood tests, I was given an appointment with a consultant. I was told I had Myeloma. I had never even heard of Myeloma, and very astonished to find it was cancer of the plasma cells within the bone marrow. I was even more shocked to discover that it was incurable, and life expectancy was dependant on how aggressive the cancer was. I was to be monitored for the next three months to determine the rate of progression.

As Judi and I were going on a holiday in May, and I had no idea of my longevity, I chose not to mention it, yet.

We did go on our holiday to Oxford, followed by two weeks in Dorset, doing house sitting for our friends Nonie and Albert.

On our return from Dorset, I was back at EDGH for another blood test, a nuclear medicine scan, and an MRI scan. A week later I was told that the Myeloma was advancing slowly, which meant I should live for a few years, rather than a few months. I was also booked in for similar tests two months later.

When I returned home, I told Judi that I had "borderline" Myeloma, but not the probable outcome, as it was still under investigation. We also had a holiday in Winsor in July, after which I would be going for the third of my series of tests. The consultant had told me that the third series of tests would show the aggressiveness of the cancer, and determine what treatment could be given to slow down its progress.

The third series of tests were followed the same day, by my appointment with the consultant. I very nervously entered his office.

"Sit down," Dr Jameson said, "I've your results in front of me."

"How bad is it?" I eagerly enquired.

"Unclear", was his response. "I need another test doing,

NOW!"

I was sent to the x-ray department where I was given a full body skeletal scan, which took ages to perform, then I was sent back to see Dr Jameson.

By now, I had been at the hospital for most of the day, and feeling both physically and mentally drained. I had to wait almost two hours until Dr Jameson, and his team had received and evaluated the skeletal scan results.

I was eventually called into the office. Dr Jameson looked up from the documents on his desk.

> "Good evening, Dr Jameson." Was the best greeting I could offer. Dr Jameson looked relatively happy, in a bemused sort of way.
>
> "We have been evaluating your results, Jeff." He said, "And there is no visible sign of any cancer in the plasma cells in your bone marrow! We don't know why, but it has gone!"

He asked me to return to the hospital to repeat the tests in a few months' time, but assured me that it is very unlikely anything untoward would be found, based on the results he was currently looking at.

I was overjoyed, to say the least! The tests were repeated in July, and again in September, and, as Dr Jameson predicted, everything was fine! Dr Jameson was still a little puzzled, and told me he had never encountered this before.

From investigations I have made since this episode, I have discovered that there are three stages of development of Myeloma, and the First Stage is controllable with appropriate medication, which could control the cancer for many years. I have still not found any documentation which has shown that even the First Stage is curable, nor have I come across anything which says that Myeloma can self-heal!

I guess I was just very lucky!

It was my 70th birthday in the September, and Antony and Lou come over from Australia to stay with Judi and I for about ten days, to help me celebrate it. I had a bit of a party, only sixteen friends and family there, but a great evening. I received my "old bloke" presents. A comb-over wig, tube of denture cleaning tablets, a pack of incontinence pants, pair of 'jam jar bottom' glasses, a set of false teeth, and even an inflatable 'Zimmer' frame!

Antony and Lou did buy me a great present. Grandstand tickets to British F1 Grand Prix, which was to be held at Silverstone in the following July. The seats were in the 'International Pits Straight', overlooking the race start/finish line. Definitely something I was looking forward to!

In late September we left for our regular extended holiday in southern Spain. We decided to stay for ten weeks this time, but have a couple of mini-holidays within the holiday.

After we had been in Spain for about four weeks, we decided to visit a place we had been told about, called Merida, which was purported to have the best Roman ruins in Europe, even better than in Italy!

We booked a hotel on the outskirts of town for a four-day visit. Merida was in the middle of nowhere, being over 200 miles south-west of Madrid, and 250 miles north of the south coast, where we were staying.

"Why did the Romans want to stay there?" I asked myself'

A little research uncovered the reason, actually two reasons. Firstly, it was a huge goldmining area, and gold had been mined from the area for at least a thousand years before the Romans conquered the area in the first century BC. In 25BC the Romans decided to build a settlement to protect the bridge over the river Guadiana, over which the gold, which the Romans now mined, was transported.

The second reason was because the Romans really liked the climate, and many soldiers decided to live there for their retirement! The name Merida is actually derived from the old Latin word for 'retired'!

We drove through town to our hotel two miles away. The hotel was beautiful, but the town didn't seem appealing at all!

> "Why are we here?" Judi enquired of me. "The town looks a dump!"
>
> "Can't disagree with you there!" I responded. "We will get unpacked and drive into town for something to eat and drink, and have a poke about."
>
> "Seems a good idea." Judi agreed.

We had a rest for an hour and set off back into town. It was about 7pm, and getting dark. Almost everywhere was closed, but we found a small bar which had tapas and good wine, so we were happy. We stayed for a couple of hours before heading back to the hotel, and decided to return to the town in the morning.

We slept well, and asked at the hotel about the Roman ruins. The amount of literature we were given was overwhelming. The town was absolutely packed with Roman sites! We got a taxi into town, and spent the next two days exploring the magnificent Roman ruins, most of which were in very good condition. Better than any I had seen anywhere else in Europe.

The modern town had just grown among the old Roman sites. A modern hotel overlooks the Temple of Diana and the remains of the Forum. A street of outdoor cafes and bars is the approach to the site of the Roman Theatre and Amphitheatre, which still has a summer festival of classic theatre with Greek and Roman productions. The Circus Maximus, which is said to be the best-preserved Roman Circus building in the World, is in the middle of a housing estate, although it is fenced off. The Aqueduct of Miracles, which supplied water to the town from the river is still standing. Even the original bridge over the river Guadiana is still complete and still used by pedestrians to cross the river.

After experiencing Merida, I knew why we came!

We left Merida happy that it was worth the 500-mile round trip to visit, and I would willingly visit again.

We returned to our penthouse apartment on the Spanish south

coast, were we remained taking in the local sights (and food, and wine) for another three weeks, before setting off on our next mini-holiday, which was to Portugal.

Our friends from Deanland, Brian and Jean, were holidaying in Albufeira with their friends. We were invited to join them for a few days, which we did. A very enjoyable time sipping glasses of wine around the pool, with trips into town for exploring and dining.

From Portugal we returned to southern Spain for the last three weeks of our holiday, before returning to England in early December.

We returned just in time for my six-monthly skin cancer check. I was still having these since my first melanoma has been discovered in 2000. I needed four 'clear' checks before I would be classed as cured, or 'in recession'. That had not happened yet! Never mind, this was my third clear check, so things were looking positive.

We drifted into Christmas, which, as usual we spent at home. Our friends Nonie and Albert, from Dorset, spent a few days with us over Christmas. We always enjoyed their company, and we discovered that we had both booked holidays in Gran Canaria in January which had a three week overlap.

2016 was to be a special year, as it was our 50th Wedding Anniversary in July, and we planned on it being exceptional. We had already booked our holiday in January to Gran Canaria, for six weeks; two weeks in Madeira in May; and a two-week Baltic Cruise in July, for our Wedding Anniversary. The cruise was only a week after the Silverstone F1 Grand Prix weekend, so we were going to have a busy year.

We were also planning to spend nine weeks in Spain in October and November, and in January 2017 we were going to go to Australia for six weeks, and be there for Judi's 70th, and Antony's 50th birthdays, which were only two days apart.

Shortly before our Baltic cruise, I started planning our trips to Spain and Australia, as we planned to do a bit more exploring in Spain. We also planned on doing some travelling in Australia, mainly with Antony and Lou, but some of it by ourselves.

Gran Canaria was beautiful, and the weather in February was gorgeous! We rented a villa in a quiet location in Las Salinas, overlooking the sea. From the roof the view of the sea was spectacular, and the roof also had a kitchen with a BBQ, and a pool. Nonie and Albert stayed in the more vibrant Puerto De Mogan, which was along the coast to the west of us. We spent a lot of time together exploring the island.

It was a very enjoyable holiday, and on our return to England, we decided we would do it again in 2017.

In April we spent two weeks in Dorset 'house sitting' for Nonie and Albert, who were away on holiday again.

In May we were off on our travels again. This time it was two weeks in Madeira, where we had never been before. Although Madeira is about 400 miles north of Gran Canaria, it still has a very pleasant climate in May. We both enjoyed Madeira, and in particular, the caves at Grutas. I enjoyed driving the small winding minor roads which covered the island, in particular the ones along the coast. Another place we decided we would revisit.

A lot of June was spent planning our Spain and Australia trips. At the end of the month, I had another skin check-up, but unfortunately, this one discovered a basal cell carcinoma on the end of my nose! It was malignant, and had to be removed, but this operation was scheduled for a month later, when we would have returned from our Baltic cruise.

We were not actually sea cruising type of people, our only previous one being on the Queen Elizabeth ll, for our 25th Wedding Anniversary! However, we were definitely looking forward to it. In particular we wanted to visit Saint Petersburg. The accommodation, food, and entertainment on the ship was excellent, but the trips ashore were better.

We stopped at Copenhagen first for a day touring the city. Then, after a few more days at sea, we arrived in Stockholm. My favourite thing there was the Ice Bar, which as the name implies, was made of ice. Everything was made of ice, even the 'glasses' the drinks came in! The ice sculptures and etchings were excellent. The only problem being that the whole bar was kept at a temperature of -5 °C!!

Our next stop after Stockholm was Tallinn. The beautiful 13th century St Nicholas church in this cobblestoned capital city of Estonia is a must for any visitor on a tour of the old city. It was an excellent aperitif to the next port of call, which was St Petersburg.

St Peterburg was the old Russian capital for two hundred years before the Russian Revolution, Moscow becoming the capital in 1922, of what then became the USSR. The architecture of St Petersburg was outstanding! My two favourite places were "Saviour on the Spilled Blood" church and the "Peter and Paul Fortress". The only problem with this city was the pickpockets. They were very good, as I can say from first-hand experience! My credit cards and cash were taken from my wallet, which was in a zipped trouser pocket, and the empty wallet replaced without my knowledge. I only discovered this when we returned to the tour bus.

On returning to the ship, I reported to the Bursar that I had been robbed.

> "Both my credit card and my bank card were stolen." I told the Bursar.
>
> "How unfortunate," the Bursar replied, "I will contact the credit card company and your bank, and you can cancel both the cards which were stolen." He very helpfully dialled both the financial institutions, to whom I spoke, and immediately had the cards cancelled. Both companies said replacement cards would be posted immediately to my home address. They could not offer a temporary card which I could access now.
>
> "As the credit card you have been using for on-board pur-

chases had been cancelled, which one will you now be using?" the Bursar went on to ask.

"Pardon! What do you mean?" I responded. "My credit card was stolen, you just helped me cancel it!"

"We still need a credit card for on-board purchases." He continued. "Otherwise, you will not be able to buy anything else on board!"

I was astounded by this revelation.

"I don't have any other cards, other than the ones that were stolen." I pointed out to him. "Just add everything to my account, invoice me when we return home, and I can pay you." Was my suggestion.

"Sorry, sir," he countered, "it's company policy."

We spent the next ten minutes debating this issue, before I managed to convince the Bursar that It would not be in his or his companies interests to take the stand he was taking! I think me threatening to not pay anything which was already on my account unless I was given credit for my future purchases, managed to sway the argument in my favour. I also managed to get a £250 cash advance, so we would have money for the future shore excursions we were booked on! As I said, there no point in us going ashore without any money, and we had paid for the excursions on my stolen credit card ships account.

On our return home, I did pay my account immediately I received it. (Two days after our return home.)

The next stop on our itinerary was Helsinki, the highlights for me being the "Uspenski Cathedral" and the "Sibelius Monument".

Our last stop before returning home, was Belgium, where we spent the day in Bruges exploring the medieval city and canals.

A few days after our cruise ended, in early August, I had the operation for the skin cancer on my nose. It was done as an outpatient, but did take a couple of hours, as the left side of my nose had to be 'rebuilt'. The facial surgeon did such a good job, that no additional surgery was subsequently required, and the scarring on my nose is almost unnoticeable. Thank you, again, National Health Service! This proved to be my last cancerous growth, and I was discharged from the Melanoma Clinic two years later, after being a patient for eighteen years!

When we were on our Baltic cruise, I developed a pain in my groin. I was examined by the ships doctor who told me I had an inguinal hernia, and to see my doctor on my return home. I did, and two weeks later I was in hospital having it attended to. A minor operation, which involved an incision in the groin, and a piece of mesh inserting, before sewing it up again. All sorted out by the time we went for our nine-week holiday to Spain in September.

During the recuperation period, when I was not allowed to exert myself, I finalised our holiday in Australia, which was to start six weeks after our return from Spain.

Our holiday in Spain was, as usual, very good, for the first six weeks. Then the worst thing that could ever happen to me, happened. Judi suffered a stroke and was rushed to hospital. Although she seemed to be recovering, she suffered a massive second stroke five days later, and died.

Those five days were absolute torture for me and, although I could wite a book on the events of those five days, I am choosing not to, as it would be too upsetting for me to relive in any detail. Only to say that my friends in the UK offered immense support, and Brian even travelled to Spain to be with me on the day Judi died. Antony few over from Australia, but due to airline staff strikes, did not arrive until the day after Judi had passed away. The following week, all three of us drove my car back to the UK, and Antony, who was later joined by Lou, stayed with me for Judi's funeral, and for the following two months. Antony left a week after what would have been Judi's seventieth birthday.

I was taking anti-depressant tablets and remember very little of what was happening during December, January, and February, other than I spent most of the time with Antony, my friends, or in bed crying. I only vaguely remember Judi's funeral the week before Christmas.

In early March 2017 I decided I had spent enough time feeling sorry for myself, stopped taking the anti-depressants, and decided to do some charity work. I needed to keep busy, and if I could help others whilst doing this, that would be a bonus. I hated being in the house by myself.

I looked at a volunteering website, and picked out two local charities I thought I could help. The first one was "Access to Healthcare", which involved collecting people from home and taking them to and from local surgeries or Medical Centres. I did this on Wednesdays and Fridays.

The second charitable organisation I joined was Parkinson's UK, helping with their "Turn to Us" awareness initiative. I visited doctor's surgeries and local hospitals distributing Parkinson's awareness information packs, which were given to people who had a family member with Parkinson's. I did this for a couple of half days a week, as I organised my own schedule, and produced a regular distribution report.

This charity work, together with my full social calendar (petanque four times a week, darts twice a week, keep fit twice a week, and visiting friends about three times a week), kept me occupied and stopped me dwelling on my own problems.

For several months I had noticed a slight nagging pain in my groin. I wasn't too bothered about it, but I was getting a pain when I wanted to pee, and was also peeing very frequently. The surgeon who had carried out my hernia operation told me it could take six months to heal properly. He also said it was possible that the other side would cause problems within a year. I assumed this was putting pressure on my bladder and making me pee too often.

It had been about eight months since the hernia operation, so I decided to visit my GP to have it evaluated.

The doctor wasn't bothered about the pain I was getting in my groin, but was concerned with the frequency at which I was urinating.

> "The slight pain is probably just the mesh from the hernia operation moving slightly, and it will be okay in a couple of months. I'm not happy about your waterworks though!"
>
> He then proceeded to give me a rectal examination.
>
> "Looks like you could have a problem here, which is nothing to do with your hernia operation, nor are there signs of another hernia developing at the other side, but your prostate is enlarged. I'm referring you to an Oncologist at the hospital (EDGH)."

I left the doctors, expecting a referral letter within a few weeks. I received a phone call from the hospital the next day, and two days later I was being examined by an Oncologist at EDGH. The following week I had a Prostate Biopsy, and the results within a week. The result showed I had Advanced Prostate Cancer. Not something I wanted to hear!

The diagnosis was not good. I was told my chances of recovery, (the definition of recovery was 'being alive in three years') was between 3% and 5%. The same day I received this confirmation, I started my treatment. Initially, a course of medication which prevents the testosterone reaching the cancerous cells in my body, which I had to take for four weeks. After this period, I started Hormone Therapy treatment, which prevents the production of testosterone, but does not kill off the cancerous cells.

Unfortunately, after having urine flow tests, it was discovered that the prostate cancer was blocking my urethra, and preventing me from urinating properly. I was told I needed a 'transurethral resection of the prostate' (TURP), which was basically a drilling out of the urethra. It involved a three day stay in hospital, and a lot of pain for the following six weeks!

A healing time of eight to ten weeks was required before the next stage of my treatment, which was the maximum dose (38 treatments over eight weeks) of External Beam Radiotherapy (EBR), which could not be started until the TURP operation had properly healed, and I was booked in for my course of treatments starting late October.

I took this opportunity to stop doing my two charity jobs, but intended to restart them after my EBR was completed in the New Year.

I also decided to visit Antony in Australia prior to starting my EBR treatments, as I had a six-week gap before they could start. I booked a five-week holiday from mid-September until late October. Although I didn't tell anyone that my survival chances were not very good, I think most of my friends were aware.

I expected this to be the last time I would see my son.

My ticket to Sydney, via Dubai, flying Emirate's airline, was for the 27th September, with the return flight booked for the 8th November. This allowed me six weeks with Antony and Lou before my prostate cancer treatment was to start on 14th November. I had just had a Hormone Therapy injection, which was good for twelve weeks, which meant my prostate cancer would not get any worse.

The flight to the Kingsford Smith airport in Sydney was comfortable and relaxed, where I was met by Ant and Lou. It had been only twelve months since Judi had died, and it seemed strange and uncomfortable travelling alone, but I was going to see my son, which I thought was for the last time, so I was more than willing to make the journey alone.

We went back to Ant and Lou's home, where my room was ready for me, and I was greeted by their two dogs, Guinness and Jax. Antony had taken time off work to show me the sights and not leave me alone.

After about a week, as we were walking along the coastal pathway, I suddenly felt tired and very out of breath. I was unable to continue with our walk, and we returned home. Antony turned to me and said,

"I think you should see the doctor tomorrow! He is just round the corner from our house. I'll come with you."

"Okay." I agreed, after all there wasn't much wrong with me. Just a little out of breath, but it would make him feel better.

I had an appointment for early the following morning.

"A bit short of breath?" the doctor questioned.

"Yes, just started yesterday." I responded.

"Any problems like this before?" he enquired further.

"Not since before I had my heart stent fitted a couple of years ago, but that's okay now, of course!" I continued.

He poked and prodded for a while before declaring that I needed to see a heart specialist. He then made an appointment for me to see one immediately I left his surgery, and have an X-ray on the way. Ant and I went to see the heart specialist, where I had more tests, more poking and prodding, and an Electrocardiogram. The specialist was not happy with the results and said,

"Jeff, you need to go to hospital! You have had several 'silent' heart attacks over the last couple of years, and your heart arteries are pretty blocked. You will need further tests in the hospital to see the extent of the damage, and what needs to be done."

"I can do this when I get back to England, can't I?" I responded.

"Definitely not!", the specialist snapped at me. "You are going NOW!"

He ordered Antony to take me to the hospital immediately, and telephoned the hospital to tell them of my imminent arrival.

I was absolutely gobsmacked!!

Antony duly took me to the hospital, which was about a thirty-minute drive away, and I was admitted for observation.

I wasn't 'observed' for very long before I was told I needed a double heart bypass operation within a week or two. I was also told that I had to remain in hospital, where I could be 'observed', until the operation could be scheduled. This depended upon how many emergency operations there were, and how quickly my condition deteriorated. I was not allowed to go back to Antony and Lou's house and just rest.

Although I had medical insurance, the insurance company decided that they would not be paying for the operation, as there is a reciprocal arrangement in place between the UK and Australia for the treatment of major medical conditions. The insurance company would only pay for consultations and medication before admission and after discharge from the hospital, but not for any treatment in the hospital. It took a week to sort out, but the hospital was happy with this.

Unfortunately, emergencies came in thick and fast! Both of the hospitals cardiac operating theatres and all of the cardiac surgeons were working round the clock. Twice I was prepared for surgery, and twice it was cancelled due to an emergency admission. This was when I met the hospital barber! As I was being stripped off in my hospital bed in readiness for my operation, a head popped round the corner of my curtain.

> "Hi, I'm Doug, the hospital barber." The head cheeringly greeted me.
>
> I'm going in for an operation, I thought. Not the time for a short back and sides!
>
> "I have to shave your body," he continued "Surgeons don't like hair!"
>
> "Oh!" I said, "My chest needs to be shaved, does it?"
>
> "Yes, and a bit more!" he responded with a pleasant smile.

I then had the most intimate 'shave' I have ever had! Neck to ankles, everything except my back!

"Are you sure it's necessary to shave my legs and balls, I'm having a heart operation?" I pointed out to Doug, who later told me he had being doing this job for fifteen years.

"As I said," responded Doug, "Surgeons don't like hair! Also, with a heart bypass, the surgeon may remove veins from your arm and leg to use as bypass arteries for your heart, so your arms and legs have to be shaved."

I accepted that at face value, but he still didn't tell me why I needed my balls shaving!

My condition was deteriorating, and during the night, after the second postponement on the third or fourth day, I had a heart attack in my hospital bed. The only thing I remember was a tremendous pain in my arm and chest, lights flashing, and a very loud alarm, as the automatic monitoring systems did their stuff. That was my total recollection of the event, until I awoke to a circle of faces looking down at me on the operating table.

"How are you feeling?" one of the faces questioned.

A grunt was all I could manage. I felt like I had been run over by a bus, and my chest was on fire as well.

"Lucky you had that heart attack in hospital," the face informed me, "or you wouldn't still be with us! We lost you for a couple of minutes, and had to resuscitate you."

Luckily, I was in the right place to survive the massive heart attack I had experienced. I had died (again), but the crash team, with the aid of a defribulator, had brought me back. I did have a large circular burn on my chest, but that was a good trade off, I thought.

This was surely my tenth brush with death!

I was now an emergency case, and was in the operating theatre within two hours.

The operation went well. It ended up as a double bypass, one donor artery being the mammary artery from inside of my chest, and the other the radial artery from my left arm. There was no need to remove a vein from my leg. The operation took about five hours.

A couple of days was spent in intensive care, and was still unconscious for the first four or five hours. I was being intubated for the first day, and very sedated for the period of intensive care. My son was allowed to see me after surgery, but I did not see him! An unexpected visitor to my bed the day after I had returned to the ward, was Doug the barber.

> "Hi Doug, I'm already bald!" I greeted him. "Nothing left to shave!"
>
> "Not quite!" he responded. "I have to shave off half of your moustache because of the tube going down your nose, and a lump off your beard on the other side of your face, because of the canular in your neck."
>
> He proceeded to trim the off the bits of hair in question. It looked ridiculous!
>
> "You might as well shave the lot off!" I said, which he did.

This was the first time I had been without a beard, since the brief time I was clean shaven working for EDS in Saudi Arabia in 1979!

After my time in intensive care, I was returned to the ward for the remainder of my recovery.

I was discharged within two weeks, but was given a strict routine of exercise and medication, and had to go to physiotherapy for about a month after discharge.

My first few days back in Antony and Lou's house was almost total rest, and although Ant and Lou went to work, I was left with the dogs. Guinness, who is a rottweiler, considered it his duty to look after me when no one was at home, and never left my side for the whole time I was confined to the house, leaning against my chair for most of the time. Jax, the other dog, an Australian ridgeback, just slept nearby.

My son and daughter-in-law really looked after me well, and I was also made welcome by Lou's parents, Nev and Lorretta, when I was allowed more freedom. My recovery was slower than I had hoped, but then, I was impatient to get on with my life.

I had to see my cardiologist a couple of times, and eventually, I was told I could fly home, but not before the 27th December. I informed my travel insurance company, and they bought me a ticket for my return trip home on the 27th December. It was on the same time flight I had originally booked, and with Emirate's airline. This worked out pretty good really, as I spent Christmas in Sydney with Antony, Louise, and Louise's family, before returning home to Deanland to spend New Year with my friends. The best of both Worlds, to my way of thinking!

When I arrived at the airport for my flight back home, it was seven weeks later than my original flight. Emirates also upgraded me, so I had a very nice personal area with a fully reclining seat, and a Personal Computer. I was also served a lot of champagne throughout the flight, and got to eat off a real plate with metal cutlery!

Chapter Eight

What Happened Next Was...

Welcome 2018!

Although my departure from Australia was tearful and difficult, I was still looking forward to returning to the home I loved, and the greatest friends in the World.

My first doctor's appointment was two days after I returned home, and I had three further appointments in the next week. One was a follow up to check out the progress of my TURP operation, which I had had about five months previously; another was for my Hormone Therapy injection; the third was with a cardiologist to check how recovery from my heart bypass was doing, and the fourth was with my oncologist.

I was also given a 'whole body' X-Ray, which gave me a surprise!

> "Hello Mr Covelle," the radiographer greeted me. "If you could just take off your outer garments, and sip this on, we can get started." He handed me what is called a patient gown, which is basically a thin piece of cloth with arm holes, open at the back, which closes with ties at the back, is far too small, and displays your backside to the rest of the World!
>
> "Really! You actually want me to try and get into this?" I answered rhetorically.

It was obvious he was serious, so I complied to my best endeavours. It fitted where it touched, and that wasn't many places!

> "Just lie on the scanning bed and we'll get started."

He got started, and it seemed to last forever, although it was probably about an hour.

> "All done." He finally announced. "Just got to check the im-

ages are okay before I can let you go. It will take two or three minutes."

After a few minutes he returned.

"That's fine. I've got everything I need."

"That broken collar bone wasn't set very well, was it?" he continued, "The broken bone ends don't even meet up. Very unprofessional! Where did you have it done?"

"What broken collar bone?" I responded with surprise. "I've never broken my collar bone!"

"Yes, you have," he replied, "but it was a long time ago."

He was, of course, correct. I was when I went down that ski slope in Iran on a car inner tube in 1978, and went into the fencing! It did hurt for a few weeks, but I never went to hospital about it, and it had healed by itself.

After my tests and X-Ray, the cardiologist and the oncologist had a meeting to determine my next stage of treatment for my prostate cancer. The decision was made to delay the start date for my thirty-eight EBR sessions by five months, to allow my body to recover from the trauma of open-heart surgery. The hormone therapy treatment I was receiving would successfully prevent the spread of the cancer for at least six months, but not eradicate it, so the delay was not considered detrimental to my progress.

At this time, I also contacted the two charities I was working with the previous year and offered my services again. My offer was declined on both cases. The reason given was similar from both. It was the combination of my age (I was then 72 years old), and my recent heart surgery, which meant I was uninsurable to drive on a commercial basis, although I was not actually paid for any work I did. The fact that my EBR treatment was continuous for eight weeks, also influenced their decisions, I think.

My friends, Cliff and Sandy; Brian and Jean; Dave and Hazel; and Keith and Elaine, all continued to be as supportive as they had been since Judi's death, and I always had someone to turn to, and I was never alone, unless I wanted to be. However, it had been a year and a half since Judi had passed away, and I always felt 'odd' when with my friends, who are all couples. I also felt I would like to meet ladies in a similar situation to me, who would like company for events which we would both feel more comfortable with, as a couple. I loved eating out, but not alone. I enjoyed going to the theatre or cinema, but not alone. I liked going to the pub for an occasional drink, but not alone. I was a friendly, amiable, good natured sort of guy who enjoyed company and conversation.

I started dating! Initially with ladies I knew casually, and a couple who lived on Deanland Park, where I live. This proved to be quite pleasant, but not ideal, as I was seeing several ladies at the same time, and some of them knew each other. Although it was my intention to just have several lady friends, it became apparent that this was not as easy as I thought. I was obviously a little naive, probably as a result of never dating for the last fifty-five years! I soon discovered that having three lady friends at the same time was not acceptable to the two I was not currently with, although there was never any sexual intimacy with any of them! I managed to upset all three, and was told to get lost by them all! I decided on a different approach. I would try on-line dating!

Why not, I thought. We are in the 21st Century, and I was sure that older people did this sort of thing, as well as the youngsters! I did a bit of research and decided the best dating site for me was the SAGA one, which seemed to have more older people than younger ones. I looked at the fees, and the cost for four months was only 50% more than the one-month fee. I thought one month would not produce much in the way of contacts, but four months should produce a dozen or so opportunities, if I was lucky. That's if anyone was looking for a seventy-two-year-old, well-worn model!

I checked through other peoples' personal information submissions. There was a lot of mandatory information required, but the free format section varied immensely. Some people only wrote a line or two, whereas others wrote a whole page. I decided to tell everything on my free format page, so that the ladies could see what was on offer, and make a knowledge-based judgment before contacting me. I also decided, mainly because I felt so shy and uncertain about this, that I would not instigate first contact, but leave it to others to contact me. The only problem I could see with this approach was that I might not get any interest for the whole four months! I decided just to play it by ear, and see what happened. It was late March, so my 'membership' would last until late July. If I had no response by then, I was going to just give it up!

I pressed the 'SUBMIT' button late in the evening, with some trepidation, and switched my computer off until the next day.

To my surprise, I had four contacts the following morning!

I contacted all four, and after a brief communication with all four, decided that only one was of interest to me, or interested in me. This was Sandy, who I met the following day for afternoon tea. She was not a happy lady, and spent the whole time moaning about her husband, who she had recently divorced. Afternoon tea lasted about an hour, and we decided not to meet again. I did feel, however, that I knew her previous husband quite well!

The following day I bought a Harley Davidson Trike! I had been looking for one for several months, and I had seen this one advertised the previous week. Although I had owned motorcycles until I was in my sixties, I had never owned, or even ridden a trike, so I wanted one!

I viewed and bought it the same day, and even had an accident on the way home! Not serious. I just scraped the side of a car, as I wasn't used to driving a wide motorcycle.

To my surprise, ladies were contacting me in droves! In the first week I had been contacted by twelve ladies. Of this lot, only two ignited my interest, and one lived in North London, which I considered too far away, so we decided not to meet at all. The other lady, Mel, lived in Horsham, and we met on the Saturday evening for dinner at a pub near Horsham. It was three days after I had met Sandy. Dinner with Mel went very well; we liked each other and decided to meet again. Mel and I got on very well, and met on a regular basis for the next eight weeks, but Mel did not want a permanent relationship, so it never matured into one.

In total, over a three-month period, I was contacted by seventy-seven ladies. I had one date with twenty of them; two dates with eight of them; and three dates with three of them. Of the twelve I had one date with, six mutually agreed for us not to meet again, I discarded two, and four dumped me!

A couple of my experiences are worth mentioning.

Rosina was a lovely lady who lived in an apartment overlooking the sea in Brighton. We met at entrance to the pier. It was early afternoon.

> "Would you like to have afternoon tea on the pier?" I asked after we had introduced ourselves.
>
> "I'd love afternoon tea." She replied, "but we can go to my apartment for it. It's a beautiful view!"

I was a little taken aback, as I always insisted that my date chose where we met. In a public place she knew, or somewhere busy she visited frequently. This was not what I expected.

> "You don't know me," I responded, "and I think it would be unwise for you to invite me into your home on a first meeting!"
>
> "You look trustworthy to me!" she stated, "I'm a psychic, and you give off good vibes."

We went to her apartment and had tea. We both behaved ourselves, although Rosina did get very friendly, as she showed me her pieces of art. She was far too artistic for me, and we parted as friends, but decided not to meet again, although she asked me to contact her if I fancied a night out in Brighton and needed a bed for the night!

Jacqui was a beautiful, tall, slim, brunette from Eastbourne. She was about ten years younger than me, and we met twice. The first morning coffee meeting at Sovereign Harbour was very pleasant, with just small talk for an hour. At the second meeting she seemed as shy as she did at the first. She was too quiet for me and

I found her uninteresting, so we decided not to meet again.

Jacqui3 (I met three Jacqui's) wanted to meet for afternoon tea in a country hotel, just outside of Battle, about fifteen miles from where I live. This Jacqui was just the opposite of the first Jacqui I met. (I never actually met Jacqui2, as we decided we were not compatible after a few messages to each other!) The third Jacqui was obviously a wealthy business woman, and definitely an extravert. We met in the reception area of the hotel.

> "You must be Jeff!" she announced, walking towards me. "I've been really looking forward to our meeting. I've arranged afternoon tea in the garden. Is that okay with you?"
>
> "That's fine." I responded, quite taken aback by her very commanding manner.

Jacqui was short, about 5'2", 65 years old, short blond curly hair, a pleasant smiling face, and a little on the chubby side. Her voice boomed when she spoke. She ushered me into the garden, where a table for two had been beautifully laid out for high tea. She questioned me in detail. It was more like a job interview than a social occasion. She also told me she was retiring in a couple of months, and her husband had died ten years previously. She has two sons and five grandchildren, who she visited when she could. When she retired, she was going to visit her family more often, and also travel extensively, but did not like travelling alone.

The lavish high tea had arrived and been consumed before she finally finished telling me about all her future plans. I was permitted to speak when I wanted to query or add something to the conversation, but at no time was there even the hint of an awkward silence! After what actually proved to be a very pleasant hour, Jacqui said.

> "You seem absolutely perfect to me! I want to spend a lot more time in my country cottage, rather than my flat in town. Could you fit into my lifestyle?"

I was lost for words! Had I just been proposed to, or just propositioned? Too much, too fast, for me!

I stammered and stuttered.

"I think we should both go away and evaluate what is happening, and have a second date in a few weeks' time to talk further."

I called the waiter over to ask for the bill, which I expected to be huge, and Jacqui stopped me.

"The high tea is on me." She announced.

"No," I responded, "I will pay for this."

"Definitely not!" Jacqui interrupted. "There is no charge. This is one of the hotels I own!"

We parted, and after a week I phoned her and told her that I didn't think we would be compatible, and we should not meet again. We didn't.

It was now mid-May, and I was so busy I didn't have time to think in detail about my upcoming cancer treatment. I had a further meeting and tests with my cardiologist to check my heart bypass operation was healing satisfactorily. My oncologist sent me for more blood tests and MRI a scan, and I was also sent to radiotherapy planning, to setup the EBR machine for my specific problem areas.

I was also having three or four dates a week with my SAGA contacts, and I was still being entertained by my friends at Deanland, joining them for dinner several times a week. I was looked upon as the after-dinner entertainment, recalling my latest dating experiences!

I was also enjoying my trike, which I discovered was a lot different to drive than a two wheeled motorcycle, but I had no further accidents.

Linda was the second of the three ladies who I had a third date with. I liked Linda a lot. She was 67 years old, but looked like she was in her mid-fifties, 5'4" tall, and slightly built, with shoulder length mousey brown hair. Her sense of humour was very much in tune with mine. She lived with her son and his family, and they were building a small bungalow for her at the bottom of their garden. Unfortunately, after our third meeting, she decided she did not want a serious relationship, but just wanted to be friends. I explained that was not my plan, and I was seeking a serious long-term relationship. I already had plenty of friends! We decided to part company, and NOT remain friends.

Elena was be far my strangest encounter through my brief but hectic on-line dating period. As usual, in the morning, I checked what was in my contacts on the SAGA website. On this morning there was a message from Elena, telling me she had read my details and was very keen to talk to me, which was in itself quite unusual. Of my seventy-seven contacts, only fifteen actually spoke on the phone with me as their first communication. I checked her details on the SAGA site, and she looked pretty good, coming up at about a 90% match.

I let her call me, which most women preferred, rather than me calling them.

> "Hi Jeff, I saw your profile, and I think we are a pretty good match. What do you think?"

> "It does look a good match." I agreed, "but we need a brief meeting, just to see how things are likely to work out."

As the experienced on-line 'dater' I now was, I had discovered that a first meeting will tell you if you are definitely not a suitable match, but it takes more than one meeting to decide if you are even likely to be a suitable match!

We chatted for about five minutes, and Elena seemed an intelligent, articulate speaker, with a pleasant southern accent. She seemed very keen on me, saying I was just the man she was looking for, for a long-term relationship, which was flattering. She was in her mid-sixties, retiring soon, and had a flat in Epsom. This was about a 75-minute drive from my home, but she did sound a nice lady!

> "Would you like to meet for lunch somewhere near where you live?" I enquired.

> "I'd love to!" she responded, "but I don't spend much of my time in my London flat now, I live mainly in my other home, which is where I am now."

"Oh!" Said I. This was getting to be intriguing. "Is your house close to me?"

"No," Elena responded, "it's in Switzerland."

There was a long pause, as I picked myself up off the floor.

"When will you be returning to Epsom?" was my next question.

"Not soon," she replied, "but I would like you to come and meet me in Switzerland, and stay with me for a few days, so we can get to know each other. Let me know your address, and I'll send you a return airline ticket for some time in the very near future."

The clunking noise was my jaw hitting the floor. I was astounded.

I thought she was joking, but we continued talking for another fifteen minutes, before I actually "chickened out" and refused the offer. I sometimes wonder what would have happened if I had accepted!

I also had a few other unexpected reactions to my online profile.

Two ladies, obviously the professional types, offered me sex at £50 and £60, for a fifteen-minute session!

Another two offered it for free!

Sirlei was a Brazilian lady living near Hastings. She was short and slender, had almost black eyes and black hair. Very attractive. We met for lunch at a local Golf Club, where she was pleasant, articulate, and outgoing. She had a lovely accent, and loved mine, which she struggled to understand. We had a second date, which was also pleasant, until she lost her temper with the waiter because her order was not quite right. She shouted and screamed at him! A bit too fiery for me, and I told her so! It didn't go down well and we curtailed our lunch and I took her home. We decided not to see each other again, but I received several heated phone calls from her later, initially asking me to meet with her again, but when I refused, she just screamed at me down the phone. I phoned a few days later, just to see if she was okay, but my number had been blocked!

Suzanne3 (there were three Suzanne's) noticed on my profile that I played petanque. She mentioned this in her initial message to me, along with saying we definitely should meet, as we had a 94% two-way match. This was my highest two-way match, and quite a pretty lady. Suzanne3 was another lady who phoned me as our second communication. After the usual preliminary greetings, she said,

> "I love petanque, and I am having a petanque holiday in a couple of weeks, with two of my friends, and I need a playing partner. Would you be interested in joining us?"
>
> As she sounded very nice on the phone and we had been chatting away for about twenty minutes, and we would not be alone, I thought this could be a good way to meet and evaluate each other.
>
> "I may be able to fit that in." I responded. "Where are you going?"
>
> "France. It's a gite in the countryside." She volunteered. "It's already booked, and you and I would be sharing one of the bedrooms. It's already been paid for, but my partner cannot make it."

On questioning Suzanne in a bit more detail, I discovered that there were originally four ladies going together, so it would be Suzanne, me, and her two lady friends, in the two-bedroomed gite.

I declined the offer, saying I would like to know her a lot better before I would consider sleeping with her! She accepted my reason, and agreed that it may be a bit presumptuous of her to ask, but said she still thought we would be a good match, and would still like to meet me on her return. I agreed to her phoning me on her return, but not expecting to hear from her again.

I was contacted by Eileen, number seventy-six on my list! She was an attractive, slim, 5'2", 67-year-old, dark blonde, with blue-green eyes. She met all of my criteria, except one. Her profile said she was a single lady, but when we first spoke, she told me that this was not strictly true. She was married! I did not date married ladies, so I was a little hesitant in responding to her, although she was an 89% match! Eileen explained to me that her husband was actually still alive, but had been suffering from dementia for the last eight years, and had actually been in a care home for the last three. Her children had encouraged her to join a dating site, as she had been alone for far too long. Her husband was not going to recover, and likely to pass away in the near future.

We decided to meet, and at noon on 23rd June, we met at a pub of Eileen's choosing for lunch. There was an almost instant chemistry between us as she approached me, and grabbed hold of my hand, which she didn't release until we sat down for lunch. I expected this initial lunch meeting to last about an hour, but it was nearer five hours before I got into my car to leave. After lunch we went for a walk, then a short drive to a nearby lake, where we talked all afternoon. I'm still surprized that Eileen got into the car of a strange man to go for a drive! She was far too trusting!

Our second date was three days later, for lunch again, but this time at a pub near me. We had lunch, and I offered to show her where I lived. She agreed to come with me in my car. Although I had intended to just drive by my house, we decided to go in for a cup of coffee.

We collected Eileen's car the following morning!

I cancelled my date with number seventy-seven.

Three days before I met Eileen, I had started my daily External Beam Radiotherapy (EBR) treatments. The first few were fine, but soon they had an adverse effect on my digestive system, and caused incontinence, stomach upsets, and severe headaches. I had told Eileen (and all the readers of my SAGA profile) that I had prostate cancer, and was awaiting treatment. I had also promised myself that I was not going to get involved in any serious relationships until I was certain I was going to be cured. I travelled to the hospital daily on my Harley Davidson trike, which somehow helped compensate for the discomfort of the medical procedure.

After twenty-eight treatments, Antony came over from Australia to stay with me, and stayed for three weeks, until all my treatments had finished. He joined me as my pillion on the trike when we went to the hospital. By now, I was staying with Eileen at her house for most of the week, and she stayed with me at weekends, but not when Antony was here! It was quite an expensive arrangement when Eileen stayed with me. She had two dogs, which had to be kennelled, as dogs are not permitted at Deanland.

In early August, only six weeks after we had met, Eileen's husband, Roth, suffered a stroke, and died shortly afterwards. Although Eileen was very upset, it was not a surprise, and as Eileen said,

> "It seemed like he died five years ago. This was just the final release for both of us."

I never met Roth.

I had my thirty-eighth (and final) EBR treatment on 10th August 2018. I had responded well, despite some rather unpleasant side effects, and was told I was in recession, but needed to continue my quarterly Hormone Therapy injections for another year. I was also told to take it easy for a few months, until I had recovered from the effects of the EBR treatment. Although I am not very good at 'taking things easy', I was watched very closely by Eileen, who ensured I did!

Eileen and I seemed to be a perfect match, and although we lived 25 miles apart, we were together for most of the time.

We went for our first holiday together at the end of August. It was for four days in the Cotswolds, where we stayed at a country club hotel. The holiday was great, the only problem being the bed in the hotel! When we checked out the lady at reception enquired,

> "How was your stay, Sir?" She addressed me as I was paying the bill.
>
> "Very nice, comfortable room," I responded, "but, the bed was

not very good."

It was a double bed, which was made by joining two single beds together.

"Oh, what was the problem?" the receptionist continued.

"Well," I said, "the two halves of bed were not joined properly, and they came apart at the most inconvenient times!"

I'm sure the receptionist blushed, and I know Eileen did, but, afterall, she did ask!

The following month we again went on holiday together, this time to Liverpool to see the Chinese Terracotta Army exhibition, and see the sights of Liverpool. The hotel and bed were fine this time!

By the time we returned from Liverpool I was looking like a vagrant! I had not had a haircut, nor trimmed my beard for three months. This was because I had decided to 'Brave the Shave', which was a shaving of the head (and in my case, chin) in public, in aid of Macmillan Cancer Support. This event took place at 'The Inn on the Park', which is on Deanland Wood Park. The shave was carried out by Eileen, who used to be a hairdresser, and raised about £700.

Eileen and I went on holiday again in November, this time to Lanzarote. A very enjoyable ten days in the sun. We were really getting to know each other now, and decided that we were definitely in love, and made for each other. Eileen met my friends, who she immediately liked, and who liked her. I met Eileen's friends and family, who liked me also, but were concerned about Eileen getting hurt, should the relationship break up. They were, understandably, a little apprehensive.

Time rolled along, and it was soon Christmas again. Eileen and I spent Christmas together at my house, just the two of us. We then spent New Year's Eve at Brian and Jeans house with Cliff and Sandy, and Dave and Hazel. It did seem a little strange to me, being part of the group of eight again. Seven had never seemed a good number, and Eileen had made me complete again. She was also an unattached lady now, which I felt more comfortable with.

I had met both of Eileen's sons who lived in the area. Neil was married with three children, and his brother Sean was a single guy. I had not met Eileen's third son, Jamie, who was married with three children, and lived in Devon. We decided to visit Jamie in February, so he could meet me. The visit went very well, and although Jamie was initially a little wary of me, he seemed happier about things after we had met face to face.

In March Eileen and I decided we would like to live together in my house. This was a very difficult decision for Eileen to make, as she had two dogs, which would have to be rehomed, as dogs are not permitted on Deanland Wood Park. Eileen's house was put on the market in March, about the same time as we went on a weeks' holiday to the New Forest.

One of the dogs was rehomed with a friend of Eileen's in West Sussex, and the other was to go to her son Jamie, after he had moved into his new, larger house in Taunton. Eileen's house sold in about six weeks, and Eileen moved in with me in late April, just after we had returned from a weeks' holiday in Shaftsbury.

It was Early May, and Eileen was washing up after lunch. As usual, I was hanging about 'helping'. I grabbed her from behind, wrapped my arms around her waist, and said,

"I think we should get married!"

We had only known each other for less than ten months, and I expected her to say it was too soon. To my astonishment she replied,

"You mean get engaged?"

"Yes, at least, to start with." Was my response.

"What a place to propose!!" Eileen responded, "While I am washing up the dishes! Yes, I accept!"

I did actually propose properly later that afternoon. A couple of days later we bought an engagement ring, and also ordered two wedding rings for the future.

◆ ◆ ◆

We decided to get married, probably the following Spring, at Lewes Registry Office.

After a week, I decided that it would be romantic to get married on a 'significant' day, so, with difficulty, I arranged our wedding for noon on 23rd June. A year, to the minute, since we first met! It was not an easy task to arrange with the Registrar, as they 'preferred not to have weddings on Sundays!'

Our wedding was a very small affair, with only our eight closest friends being invited. Brian and Jean, Cliff and Sandy, Dave and Hazel, and, Keith and Elaine. After the ceremony we had lunch at the Deans Place Hotel in Alfriston. Our honeymoon was house sitting for Eileen's friend who had adopted one of her dogs, as they were on holiday, and we had arranged to house sit before we had decided to get married!

Our Wedding Party took place the following Saturday, and we had about seventy guests.

The rest of the year was absolutely fantastic! We were never apart! We even did a house sit for Jamie in Taunton for a week, and we spent my birthday on a Mediterranean cruise.

In November we had a two-week holiday in Marrakech, following that later in the year with another in Cornwall.

Christmas 2019 was spent with Eileen's son Jamie and his family in Taunton.

My health seemed to be fine. No problems with my prostate cancer, which was still in remission, and my quarterly Hormone Therapy injections were discontinued in August. I was, however, still having regular check-ups.

It was 2020 !!

Where had the last seventy-five years gone?

I was very happily married to the most devoted lady in the World.

Nothing could ever go wrong again in our lives. We had both found our soul partners.

We had a great holiday in Fuerteventura in February, and were planning to visit my son, Antony, in Australia in March or April for six or seven weeks. Then, Covid19 happened! It struck the UK hard in March, and at the end of March, the country was in 'Lockdown', along with most of the World. No chance of holidaying to Australia, which had totally closed down, not allowing any flights into the country from anywhere!

Not much socialising with friends for the following months. A time of watching a lot of television, on-line video chats, and having shopping delivered. However, Eileen and I had been married for less than a year, and were still on honeymoon, so no problem for us. By June the Covid19 restrictions were eased a little, and we were able to visit friends, and Eileen's grandchildren were allowed to stay with us for a couple of days at a time.

Everybody was getting a bit 'stir crazy', and we weren't any different. We decided to make a video! It was just Eileen and I, dressed appropriately, doing the Time Warp from the Rocky Horror Picture Show. I was Frank N Furter, Eileen was Magenta. It was a good laugh, although it surprised a few of our friends when it was posted on U-Tube.

During this time, Eileen was diagnosed with sleep apnoea, which was a bit of a surprise, but she soon got used to sleeping with her mask on, and I got used to sleeping with Darth Vader!

In July the Covid restrictions eased enough for us to visit Eileen's son and family in Taunton, and we also had a weeks' holiday in the UK in August. My 75th birthday was spent with Eileen and our friends at Deanland having an Indian curry at our favourite restaurant. The following week Eileen and I went to the Peak District for a very pleasant holiday. Eileen had not been to many places 'up north', and loved the scenery of the area.

I was still being monitored for my prostate cancer, having blood tests every couple of months. Just before going on our Peak District holiday, one of the blood tests showed an 'irregularity', and a raised PSA (an enzyme which could indicate prostate cancer) reading, which needed investigation. As a precaution I was given an MRI scan and a DEXA (bone density) scan before we went on holiday. On return from the Peak District, I was told I needed to have a liver biopsy, which I had almost immediately. The results would take ten days, and the Oncology department would call me on that date.

We were again on holiday the following week. This time a visit to Windermere in the Lake District, which Eileen had never been to before. October is probably not the best time to visit the Lakes, but the weather was good to us, and the views were spectacular. We stayed in a very small wooden lodge on the edge of Lake Windermere. It was so small that we had to get into bed from the bottom, as there was no space at either side of the double bed, but the view of the lake was beautiful!

In the middle of our Windermere holiday, on the 14th October, I received the phone call from the hospital about the result of my biopsy. We were driving, but I stopped in a car park to take the call on my mobile in the car. The phone rang.

"Hello." I answered. I did, of course, know who it was.

"Hello, this is Dr Magnusson, Oncology department. Am I speaking to Mr Covelle?" the voice asked.

"Yes," I responded, "do you have the biopsy result for me?"

"I have." Continued Dr Magnusson. "it's positive."

I sighed with relief, before he resumed. "You do have liver cancer, which has metastasized from your prostate cancer."

A negative result is a good result, a positive result a bad one. I misunderstood the medical terminology. He then continued.

"Unfortunately, it is also incurable and terminal. I will arrange for you to see one of the specialist MacMillan nurses when you return home."

"Am I likely to die or become ill within the next few weeks, or will it take years?" I enquired.

"You won't die in the next few weeks," Dr Magnusson replied, "It will take months."

That was the end of a very short conversation, which left Eileen and I devastated.

We didn't know what to do. We were sitting in a car park in Windermere, heads spinning, trying to take in what we had just been told.

"Do you want to go back home?" Eileen asked. I thought about it a little before replying.

"Not really. Where we are doesn't matter. It's our approach to this challenge that is important, and I want to face things on a positive note. I would like to continue with the remainder of our holiday, then think about this more when we return home."

Neither of us was in a good frame of mind, as we walked around Windermere looking in the gift shops. Eileen looking for something for her grand-daughter. In one of the shops, I spotted a cap. It had written across the front, "NO BAD DAYS". I decided to adopt that as my motto, and bought the cap, which I wore for the rest of our holiday.

The remaining four days of our holiday seemed a lot more meaningful as we explored the beautiful scenery of the area, as I thought this could be my last ever holiday with Eileen. Apart from going to bed, I never took my cap off. It was there just to remind me to live every day to the full, as if it were my last. Eileen held back her tears well, but I could see her crying inside. I did, discretely, contact Dr Magnusson again to try and find out more information about my condition. I was told that my life expectancy would be about fourteen weeks without treatment, a bit more if I decided to have chemotherapy. I didn't tell Eileen about this telephone call.

Two days after our return home, I had an appointment with

Andi, my allocated MacMillan nurse. Eileen insisted on accompanying me, which I was grateful for, although in some ways I would rather have censored anything I was going to be told before telling Eileen. We were both very dejected, tearful, and apprehensive before our meeting with Andi. Upon our arrival at the hospital, we were shown into Andi's office.

> "Hello, you must be Jeff and Eileen." Andi greeted us, in a lot more cheerful tone than I was expecting. "We need to talk about your condition, and the best way forward for you." She continued.

This seemed a lot more positive than I was expecting! Andi did confirm the diagnosis I was given was correct, and, yes, the liver cancer was a terminal disease without cure, but it could be slowed down. I was expecting to be told I should have chemotherapy, but she was very honest, saying that chemotherapy would probably not be effective for my condition. She told us about a very new drug which had only been available for the last five years, which was very successful in controlling metastasized cancers. I was given the option to have chemotherapy treatment, which was for a few weeks followed by a break, then resumed; or I could take the new medication, which was for every day, for as long as your body could tolerate it. For some people the toleration period was a few months, but she did have one patient who had been taking it for the five years, since it was introduced.

Andi went on to explain the side effects, which were not pleasant, but did emphasise that it will increase my life expectancy. I opted to give it a go, thinking about my new motto "NO BAD DAYS", and my overwhelming desire to spend a lot more time with Eileen. I was, and still am, determined to beat that five year record!

We came out of the hospital in a lot better frame of mind than when we went in! Andi really did give us both new lives. I started the medication immediately, and there are side effects which are not pleasant. The worst one for me are the pains in my joints, especially first thing in the morning. I also get headaches frequently, and stomach cramps. I also tire very quickly.

I am also still having medication for the prostate cancer, which also has side effects. These are hot flushes, weight increase, and I am always hungry. Weight control is definitely a problem for me!

Since that first meeting with Andi, I have tried to continue my life as normally as is possible. I have my prostate cancer injections every three months and take my medication daily to slow down the cancer in my liver, and hopefully, prevent spread to further organs. Every six weeks I meet with my Macmillan nurse for a check-up, and have a CT scan every ten weeks or so. I do realise, and accept, that there is no cure for me, but that doesn't mean I can't have an enjoyable life.

Eileen and I have been on several holidays (covid permitting) in the last year. We went to Southern Ireland, where Eileen's mother originates from, to track down some of Eileen's relations. We managed to find two cousins. We did, of course, do all the tourist things, including kissing the Blarney Stone!

We also had a holiday in Durham, which is my part of the World, where we met some of my very old friends.

It is now almost Christmas 2021. We have just booked a four-day holiday in Torquay for the gap between Christmas and New Year, with our next door neighbours and friends, Keith and Elaine.

It has been well over a year since I was given my 'terminal' diagnosis, being told I would be lucky to be around for Christmas 2020! Although I have almost stopped my keep fit sessions, I still play petanque three time a week, darts once a week, and I go out with the guys for a few beers on a Friday evening. Eileen and I still socialise, having holidays and visiting friends and family. Covid willing, we hope to visit my son in Australia for a couple of months in the Spring.

Eileen and I are still very much in love, and although all my days are not great, there are NO BAD DAYS!

THE END

Printed in Great Britain
by Amazon

75236889R00144